COLORING BOOKS FOR GIRLS

Doodles Cutes

I ♥ U!

TEST YOUR COLOR

TEST YOUR COLOR

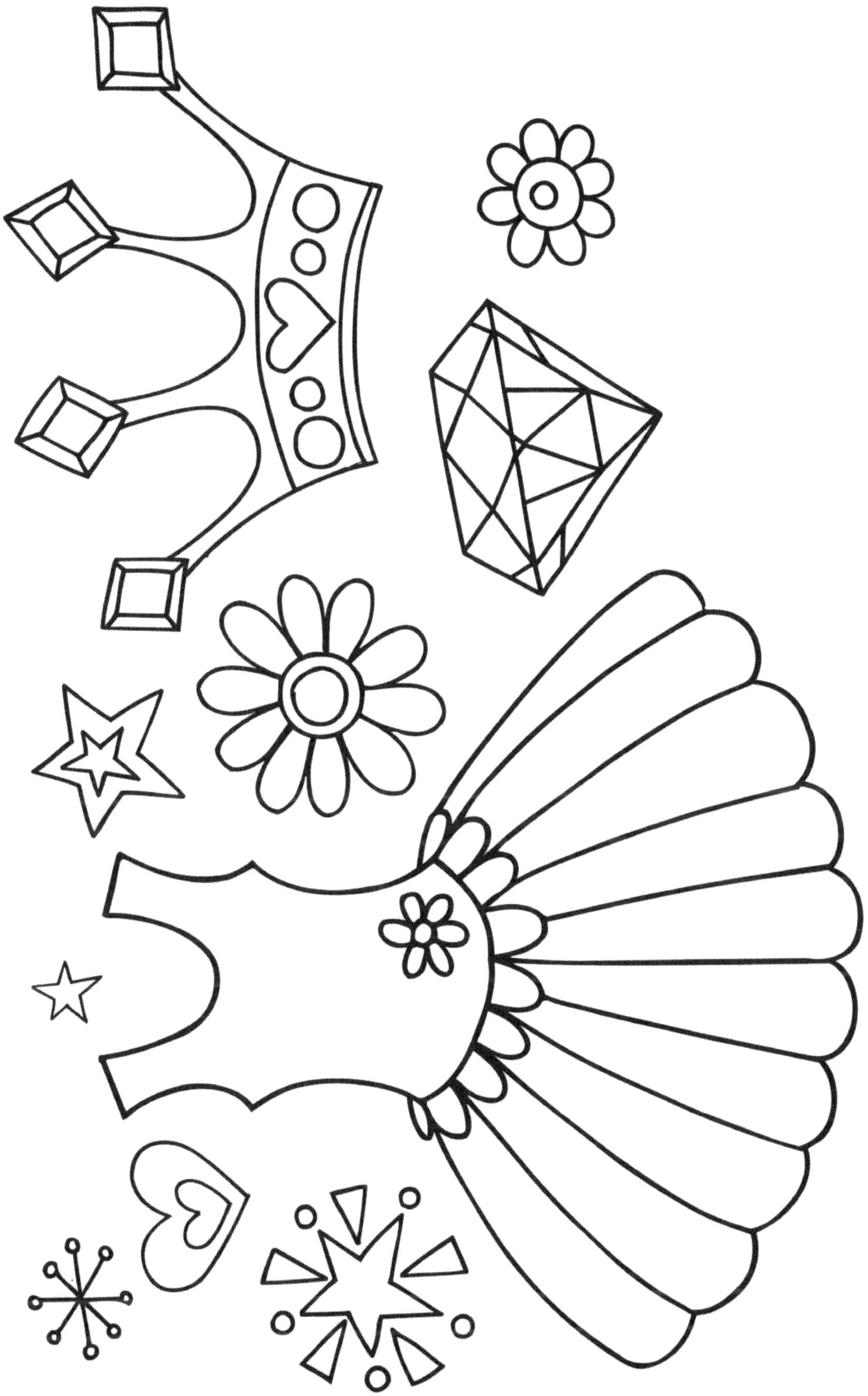

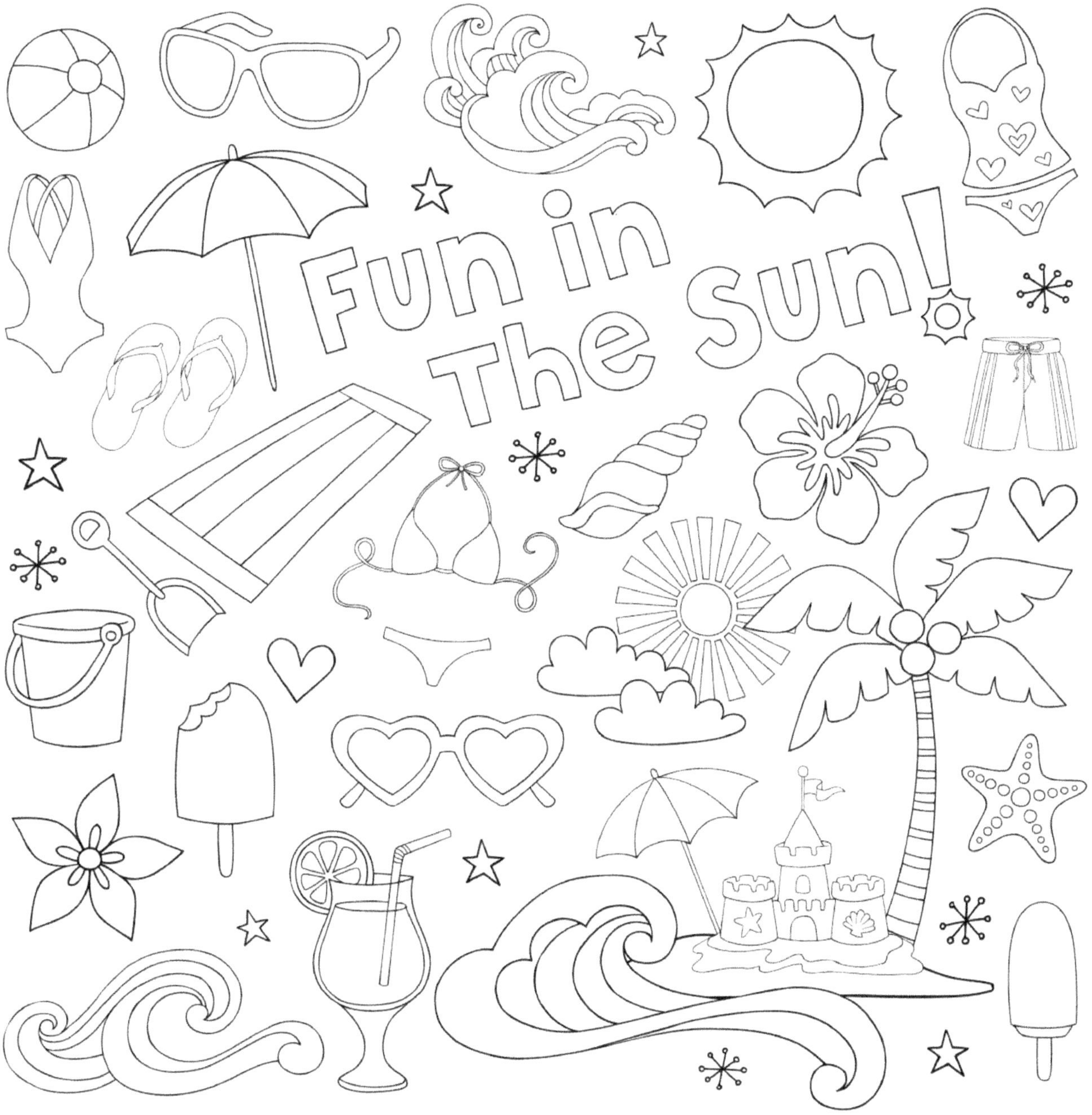
Fun in
The Sun!

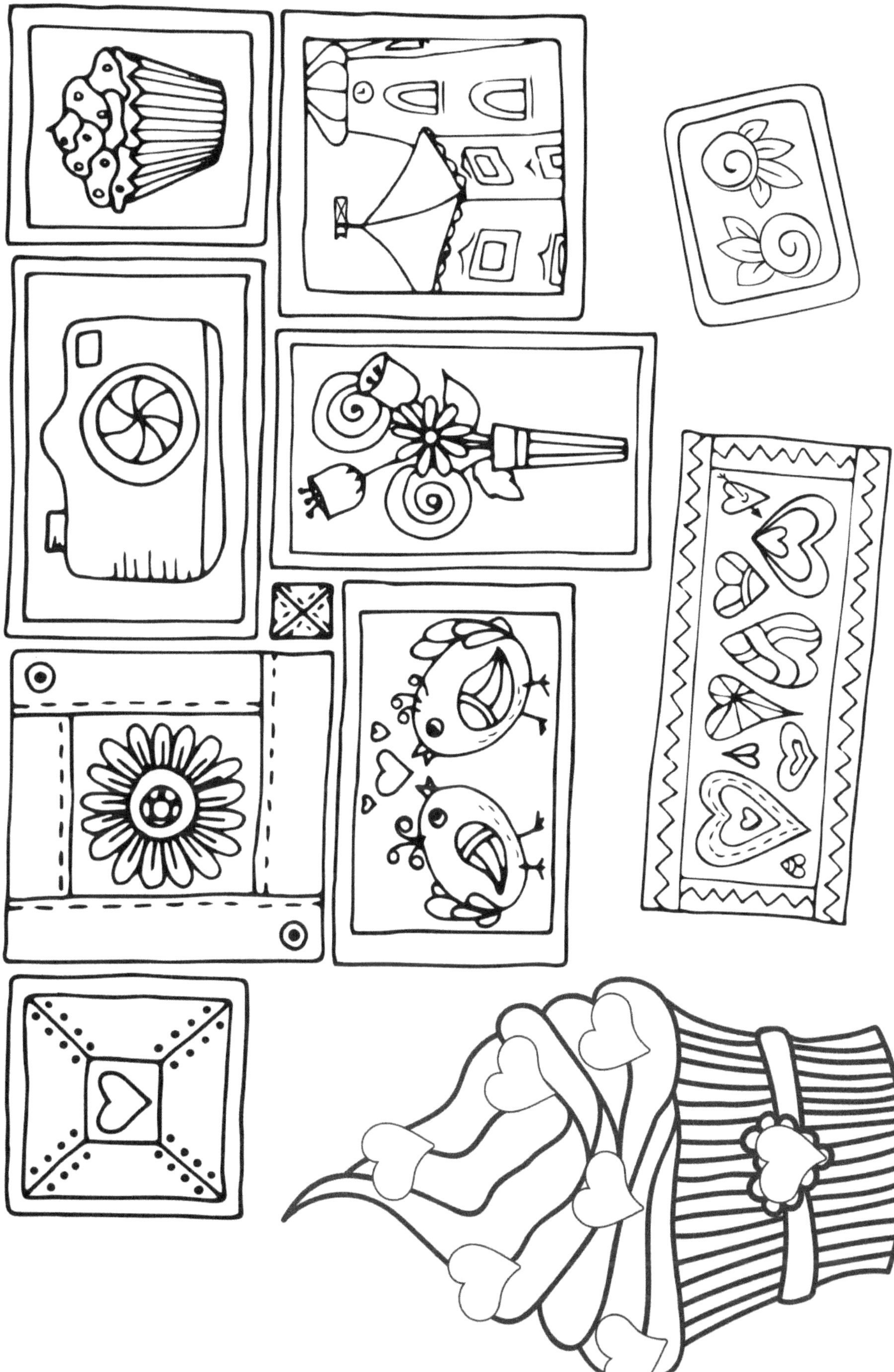

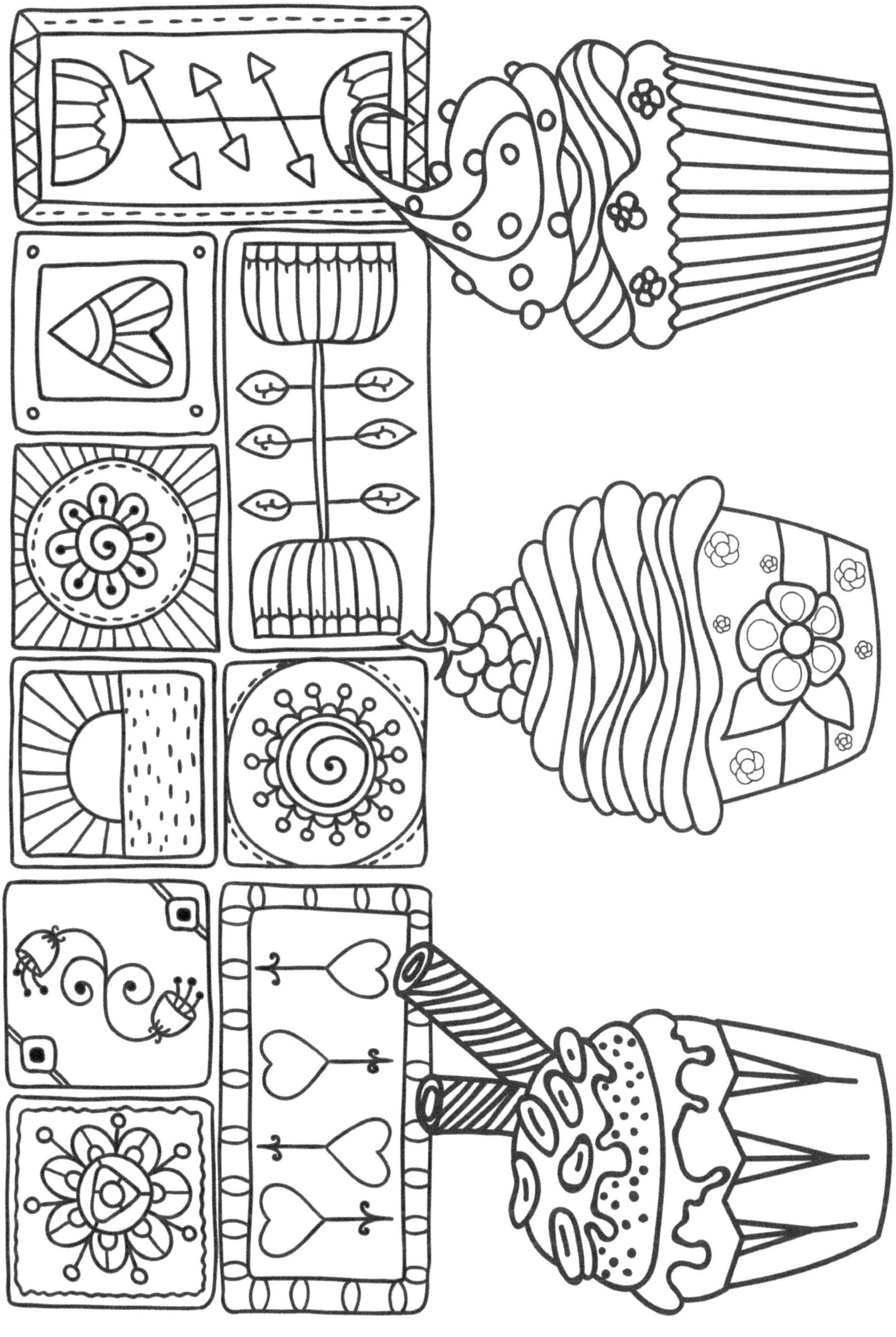

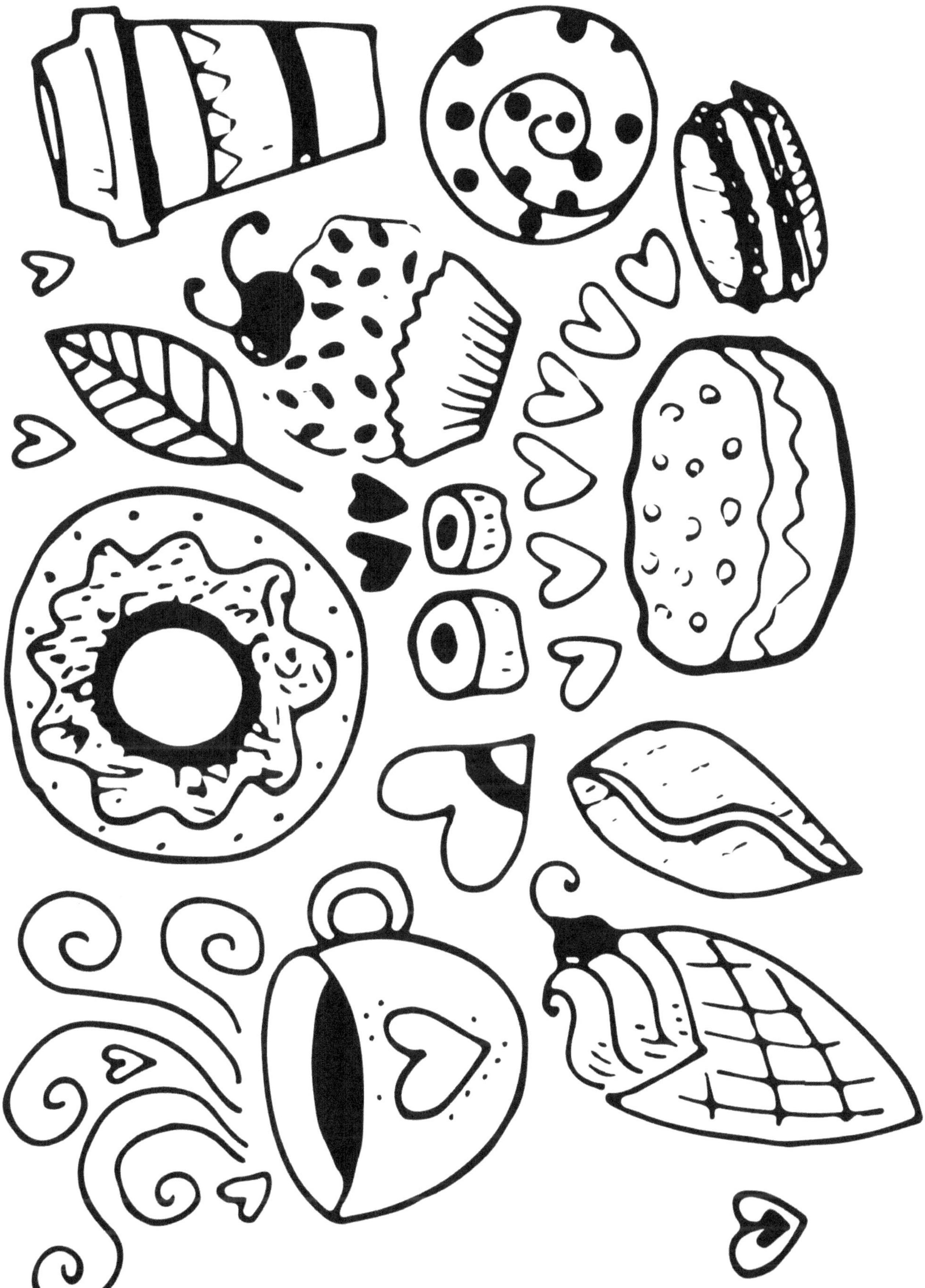

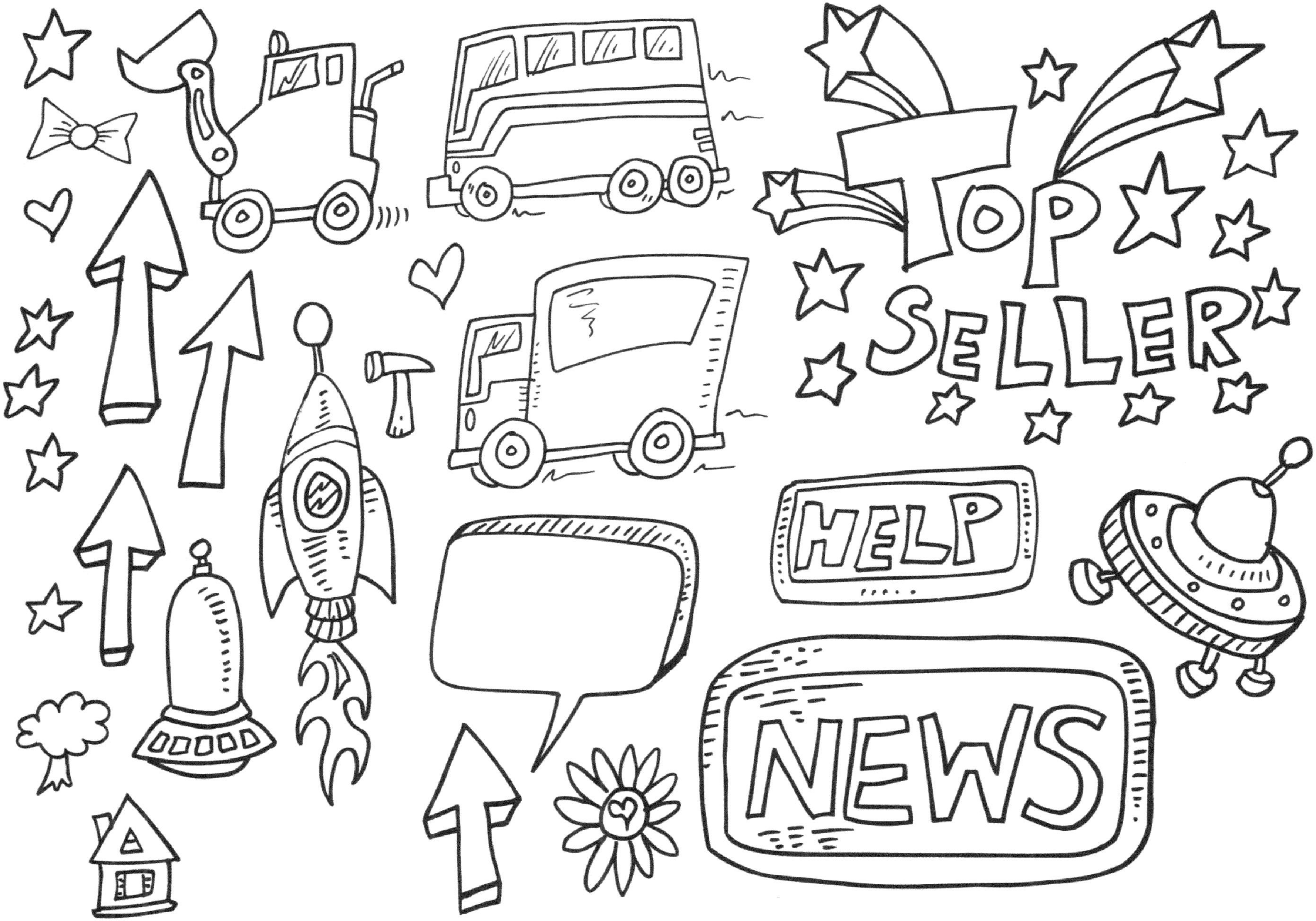
TOP SELLER
HELP
NEWS

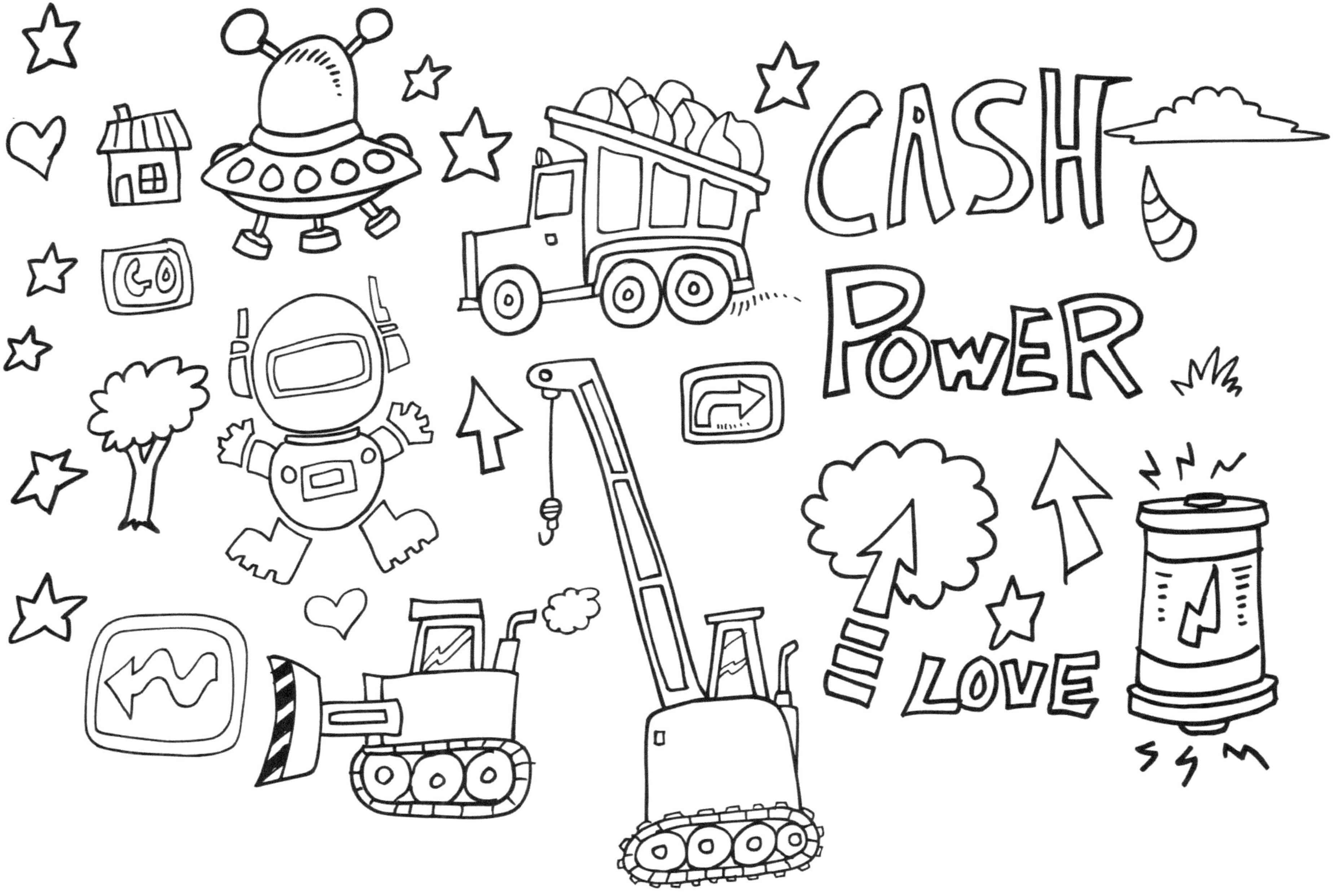
CASH
POWER
LOVE
GO

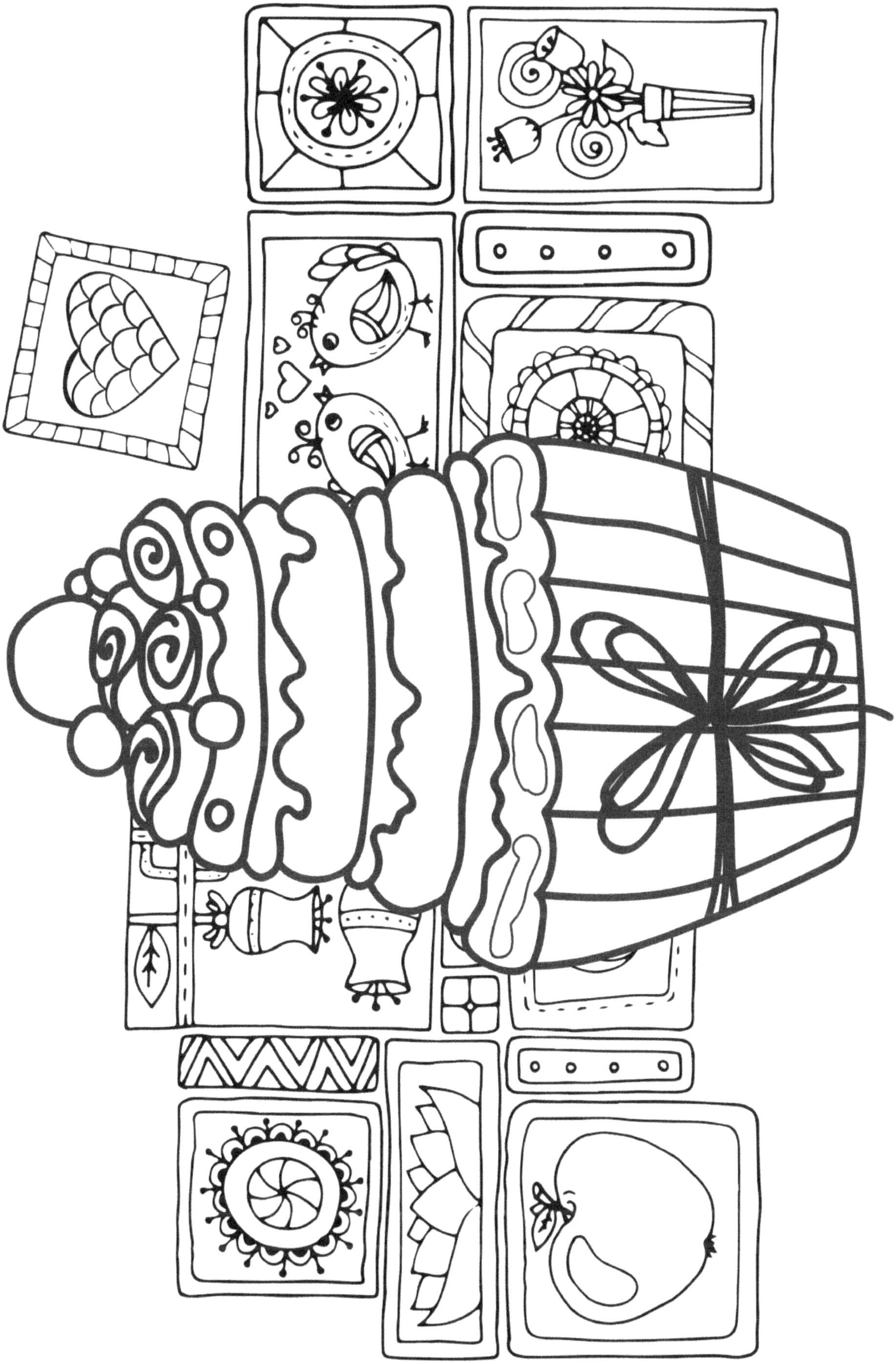

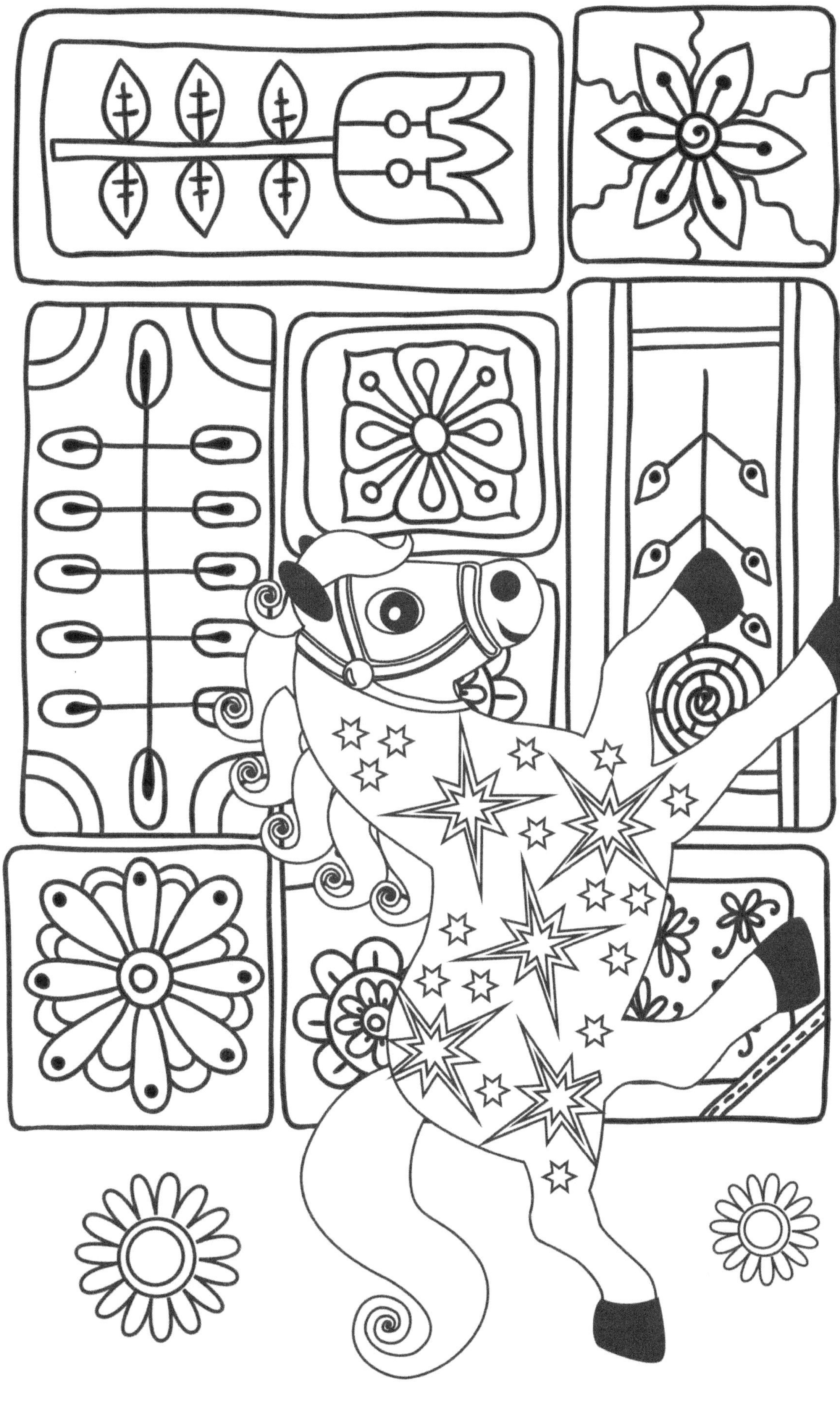

FAV

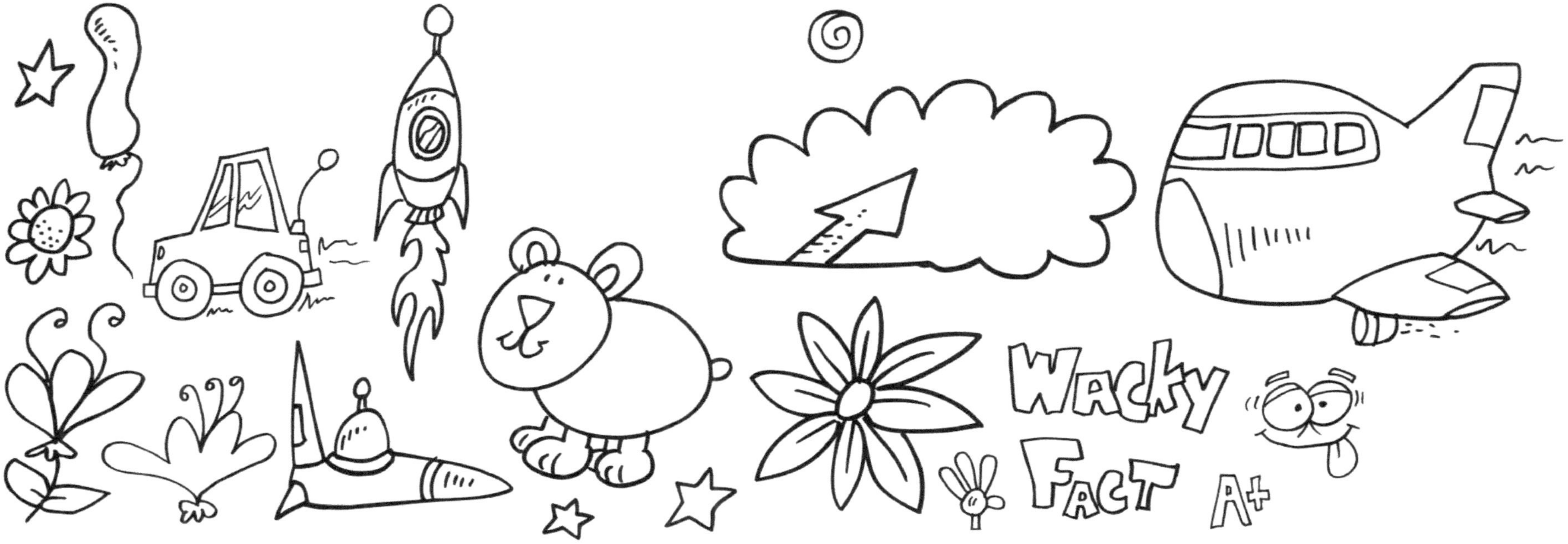
Wacky Fact
A+

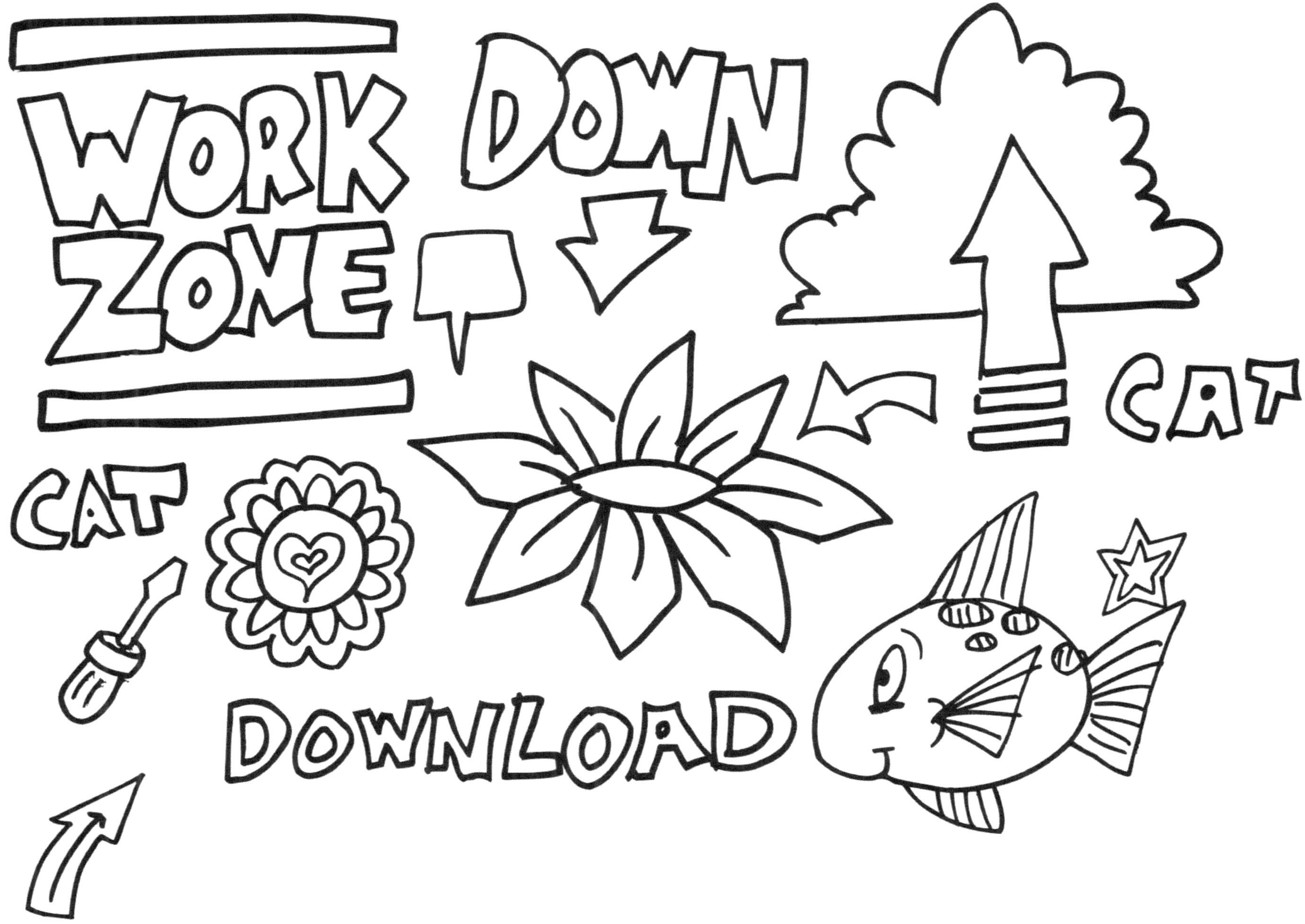
WORK ZONE
DOWN
CAT
CAT
DOWNLOAD

Like
PET
$
PARTY
TiME

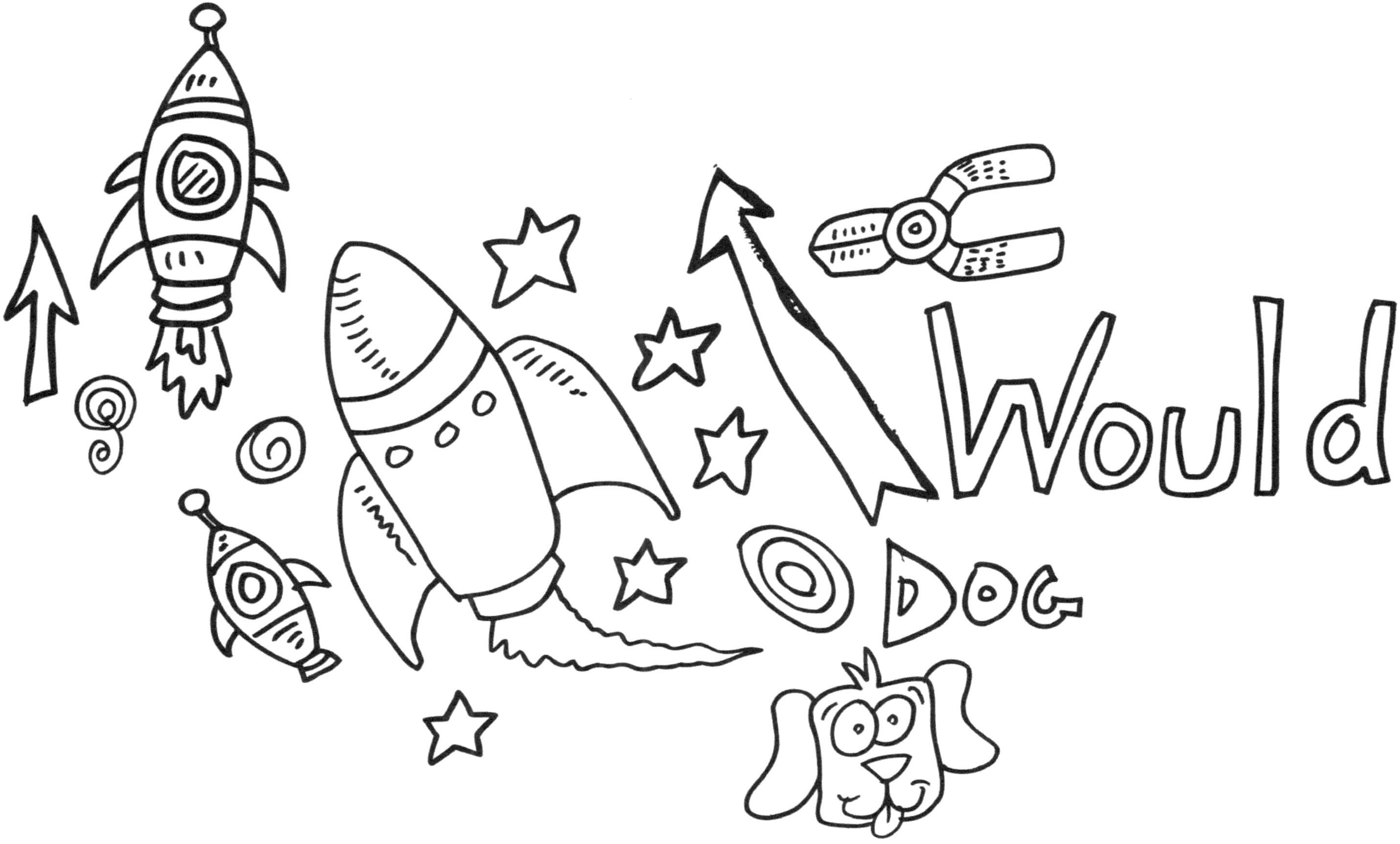
Would
DOG

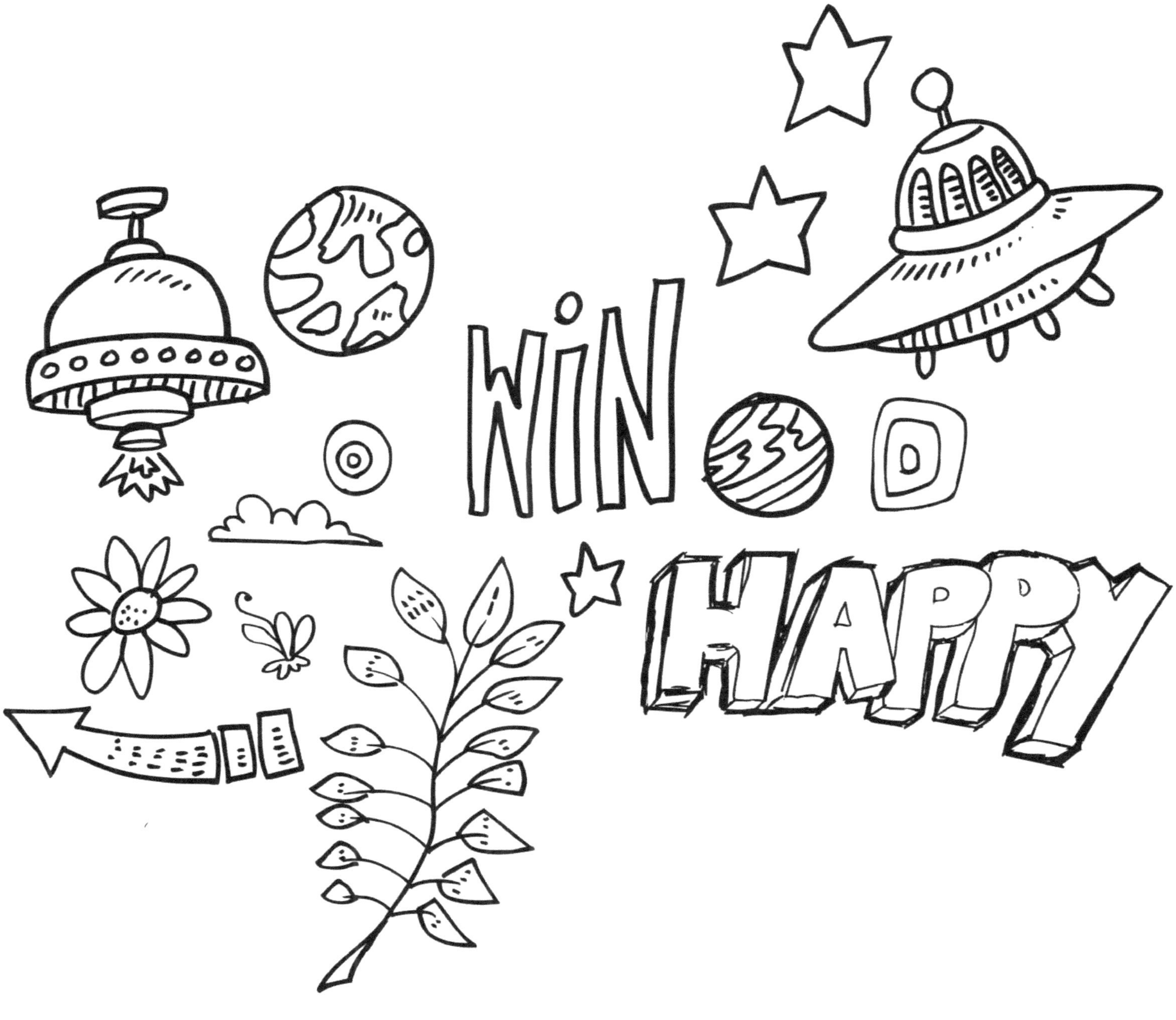
WIN
HAPPY

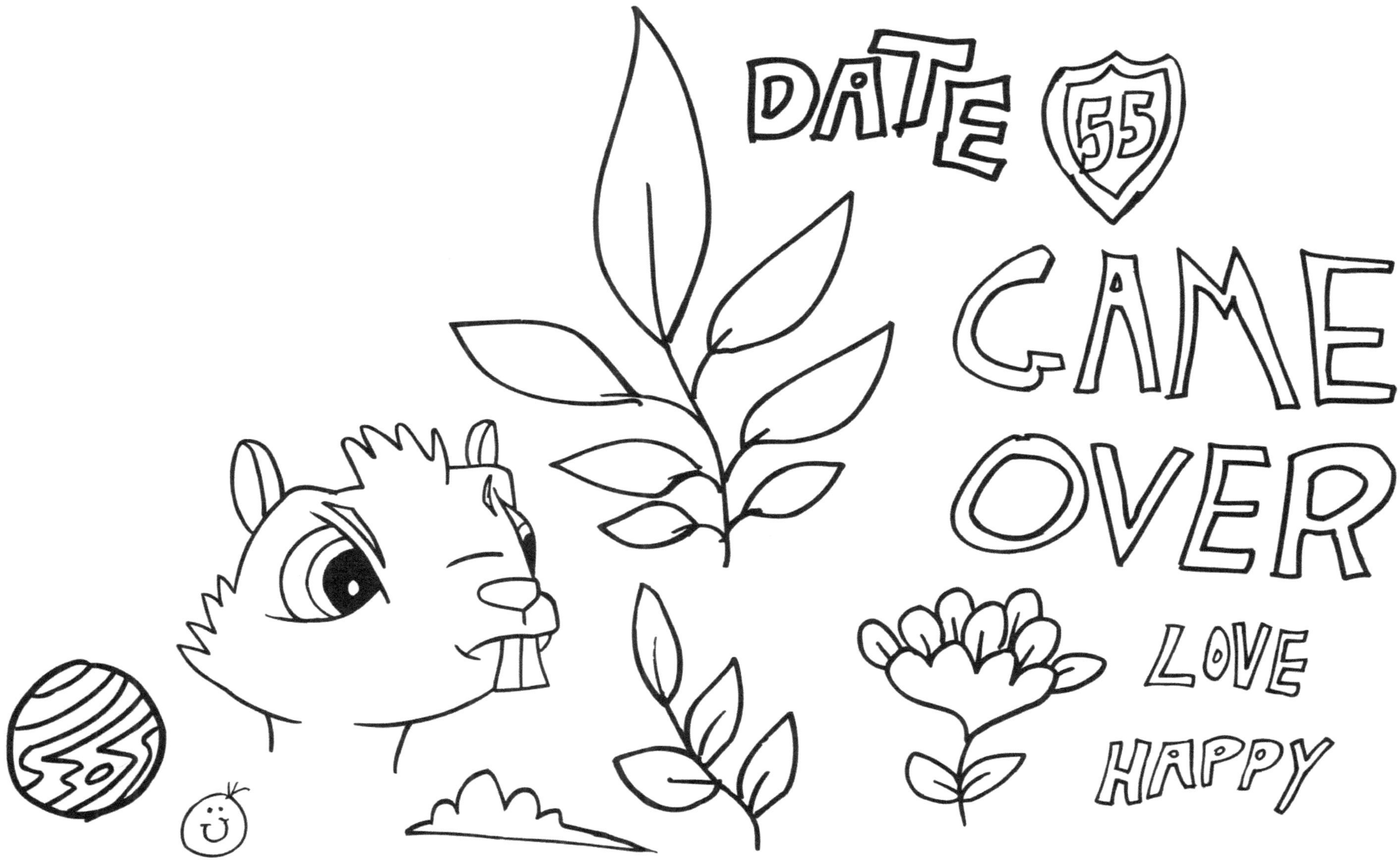
DATE
55
GAME
OVER
LOVE
HAPPY
SOS

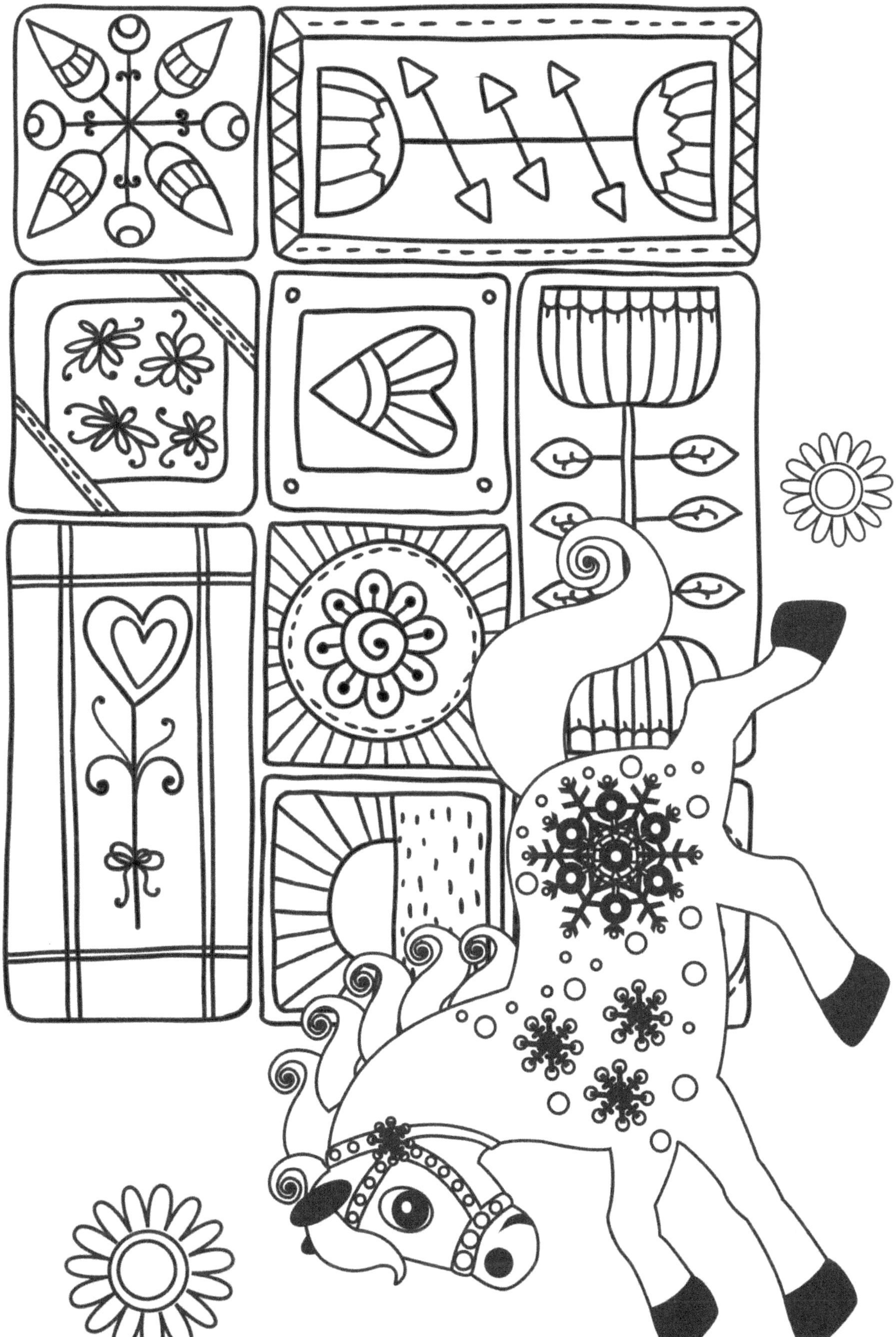

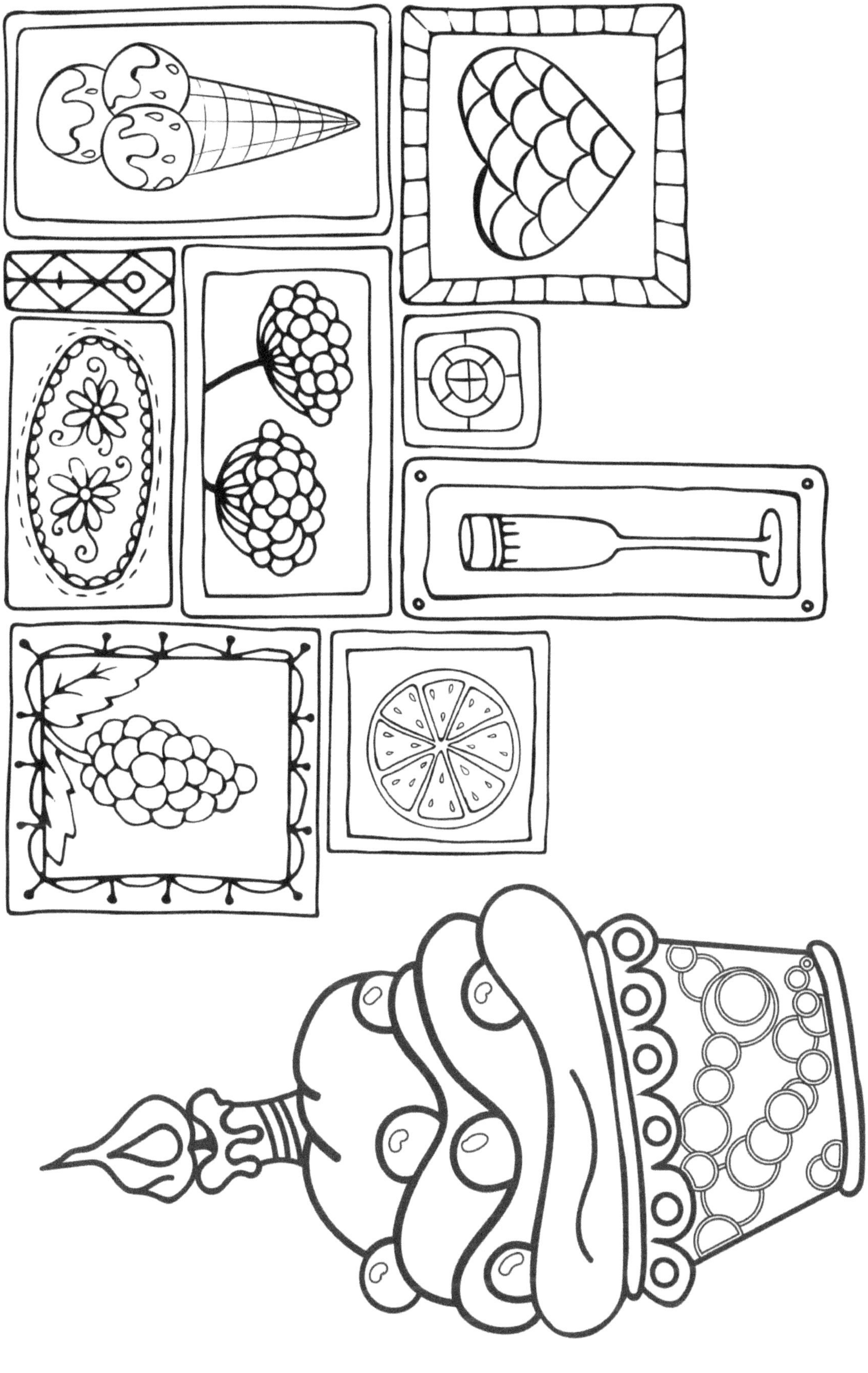

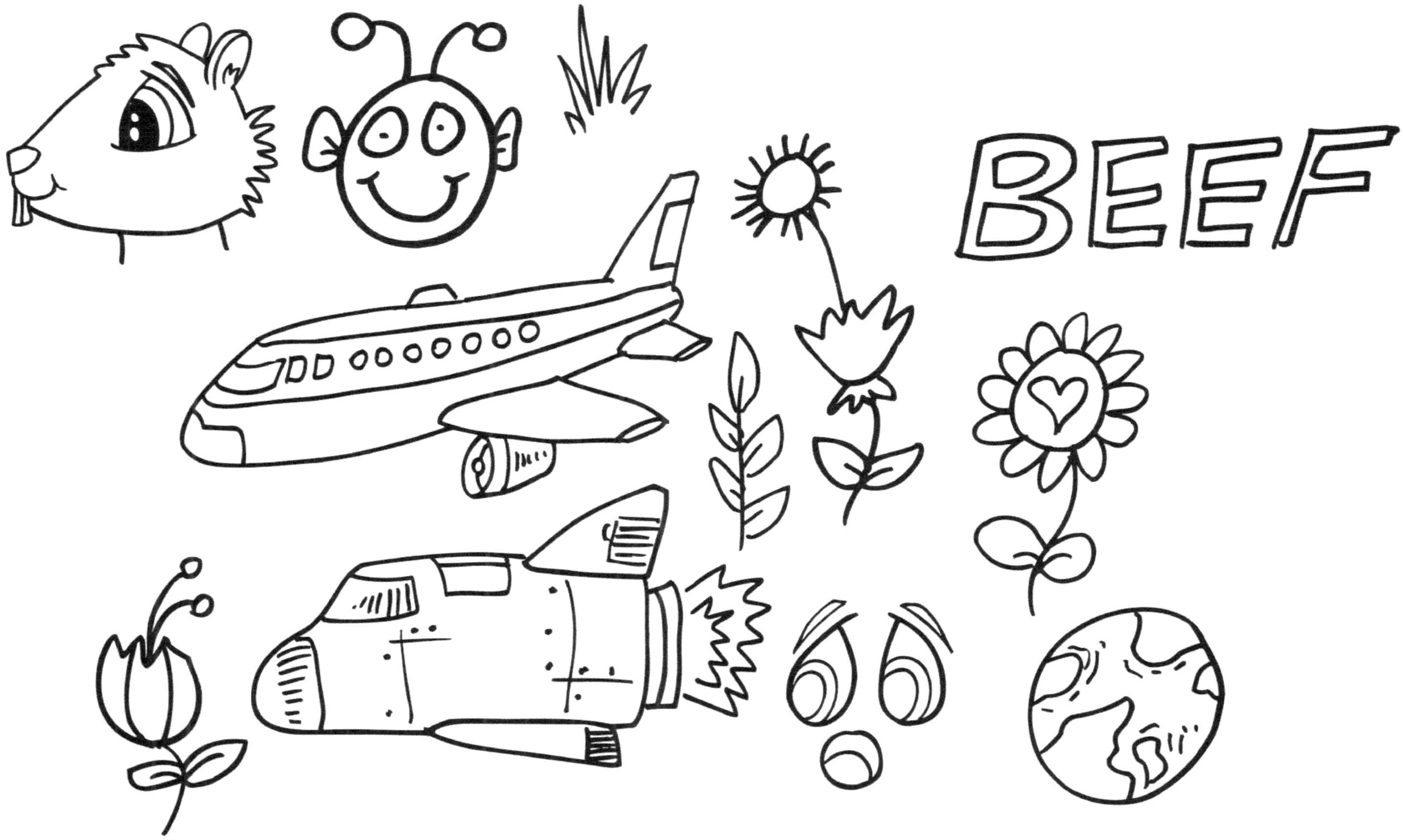
BEEF

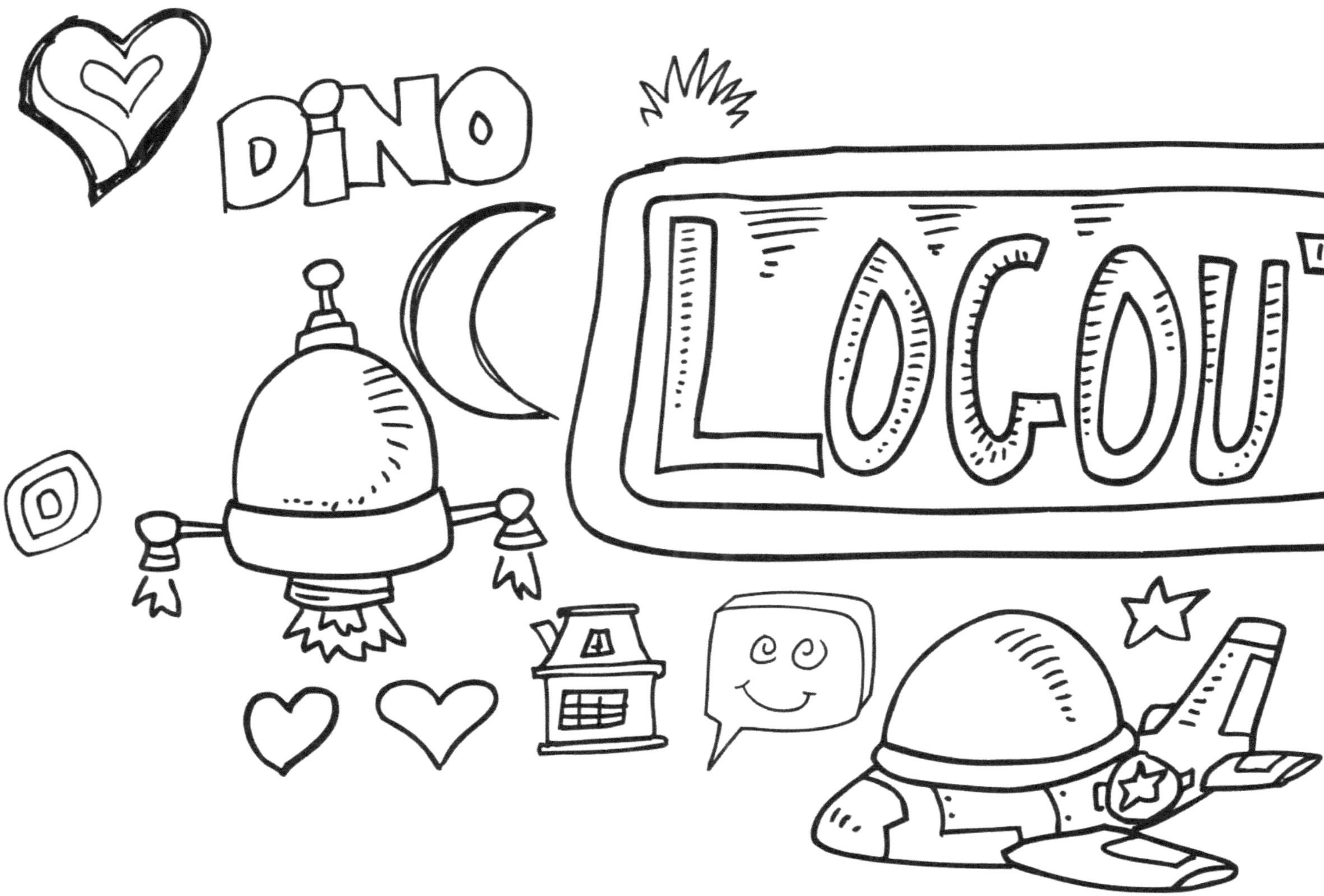
DINO
LOGOUT

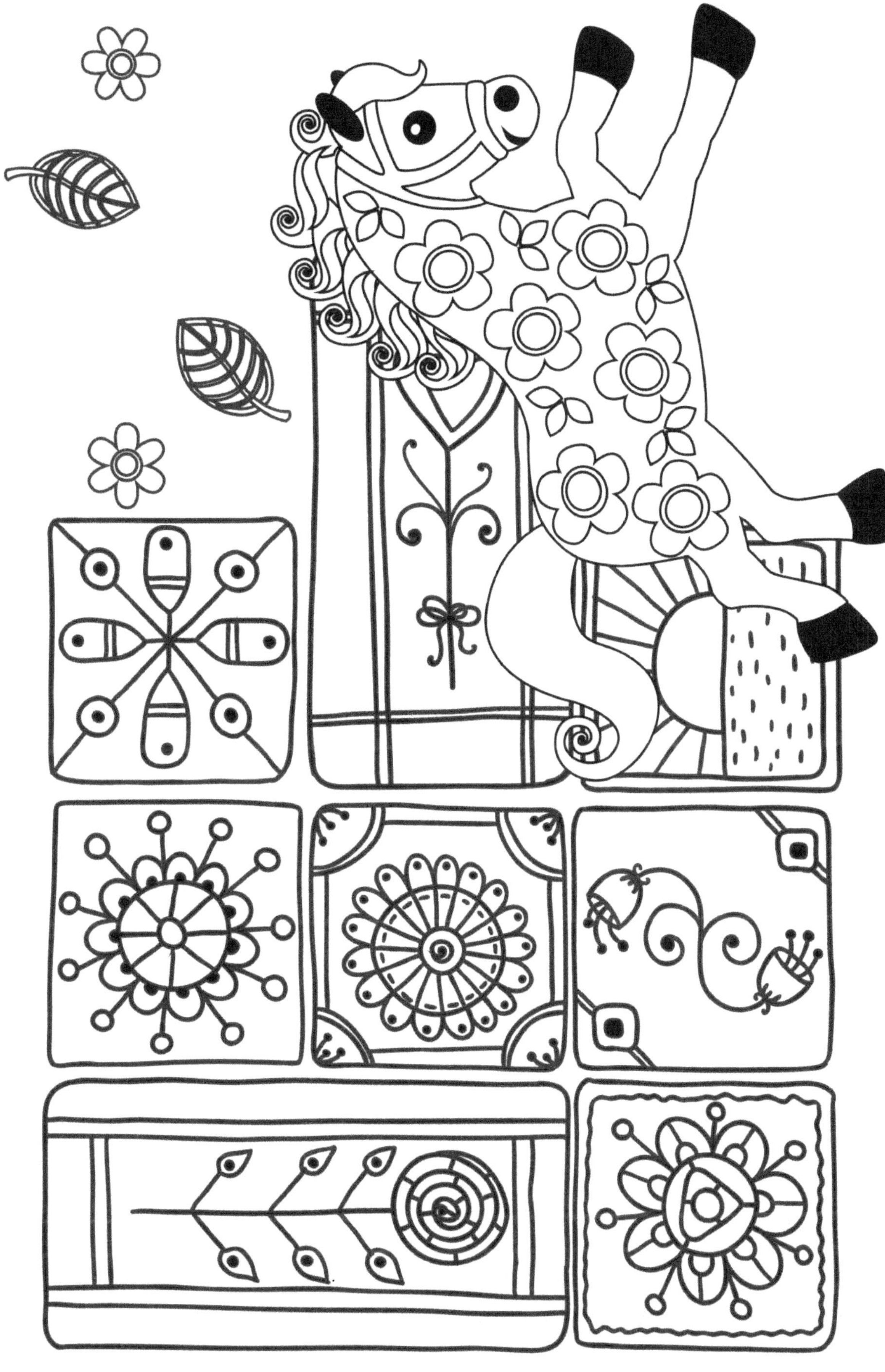

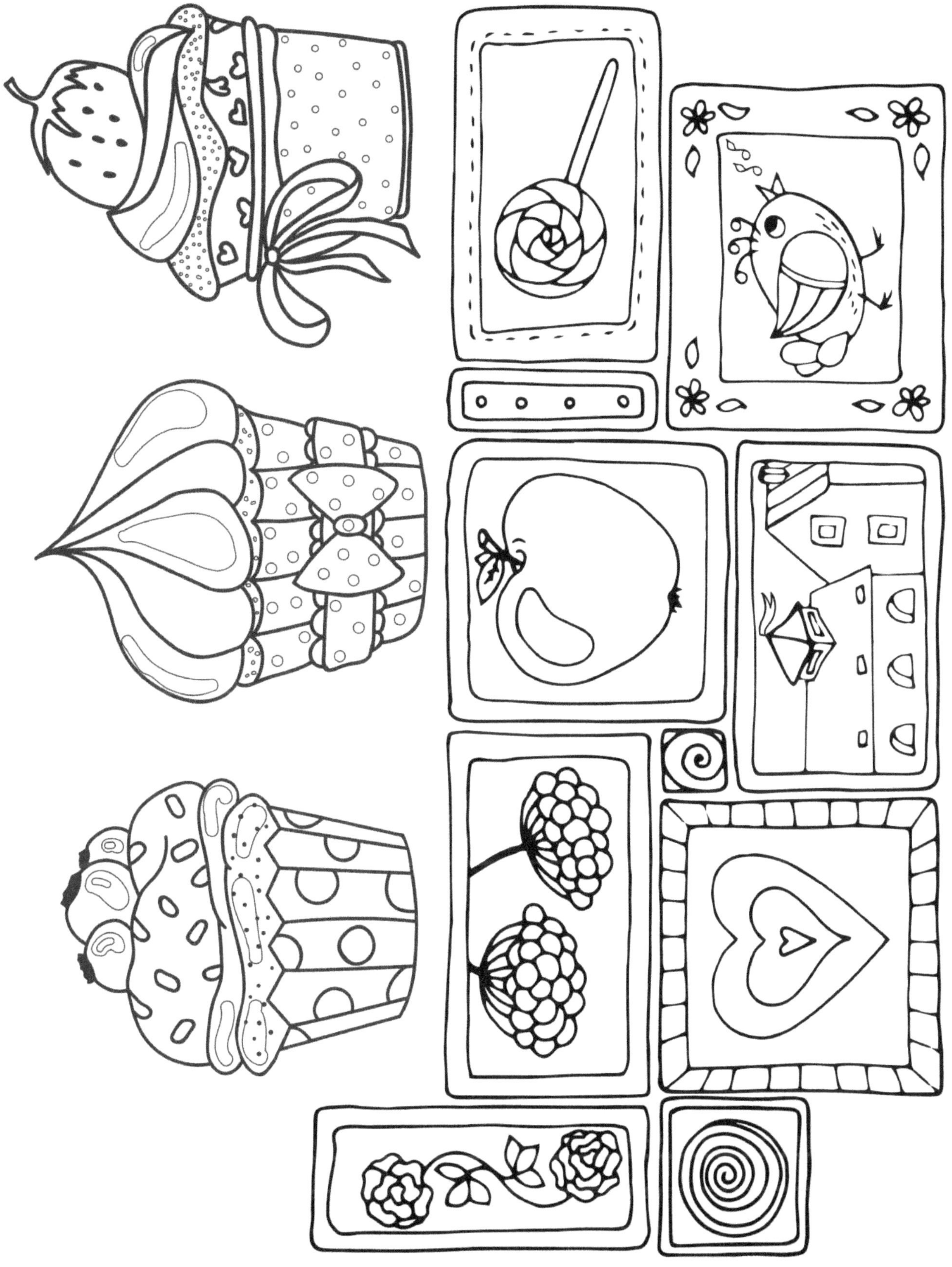

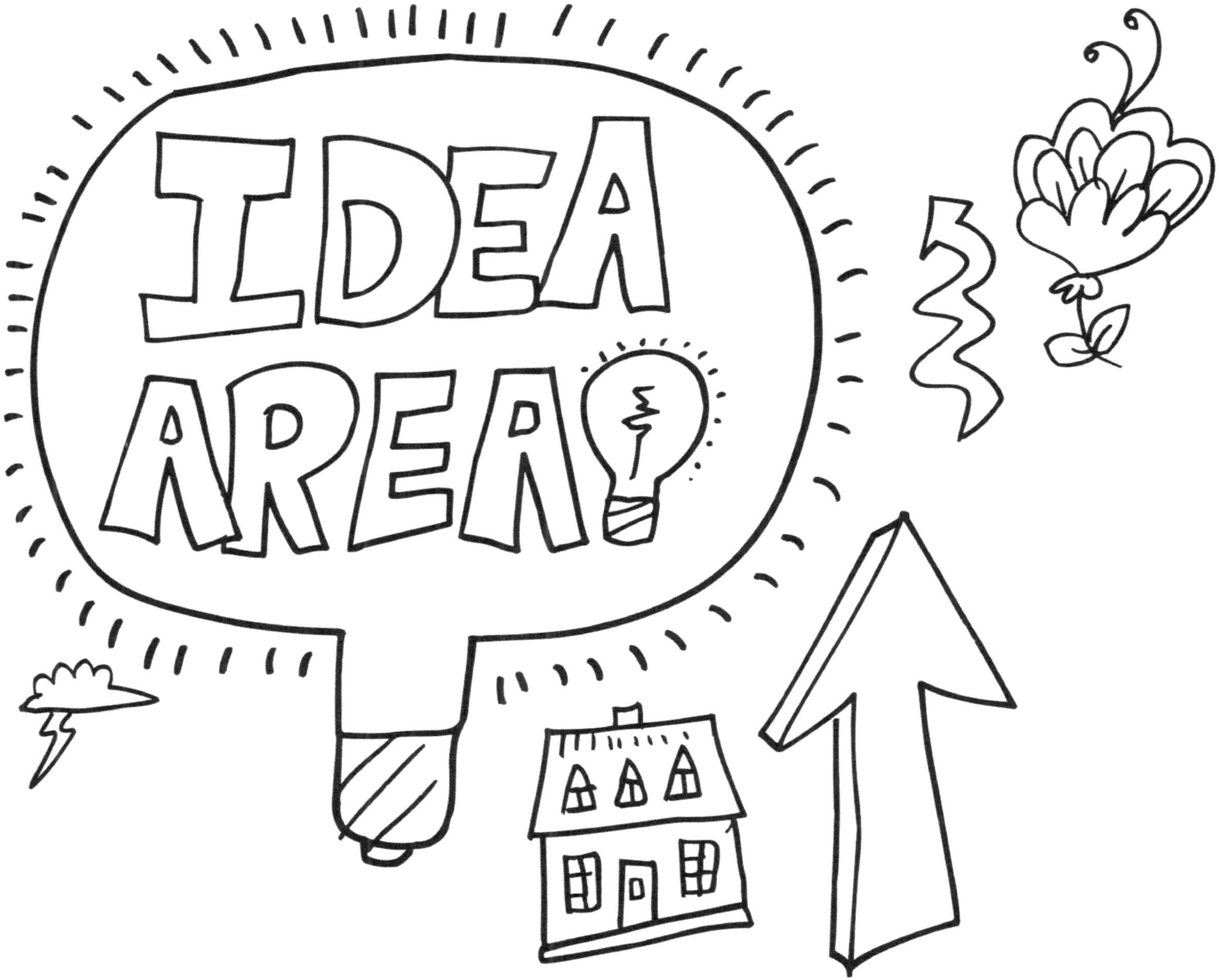
IDEA
AREA

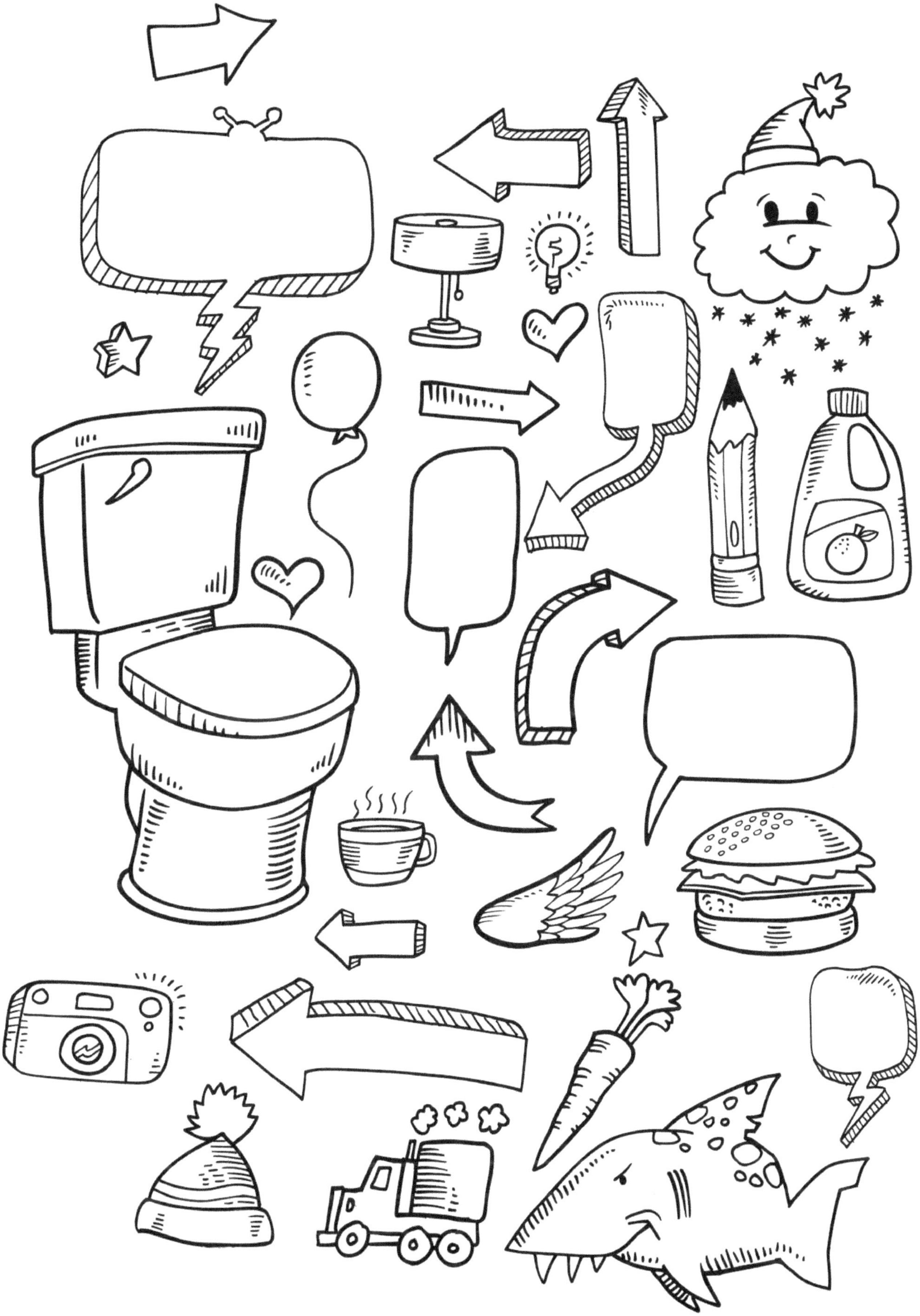

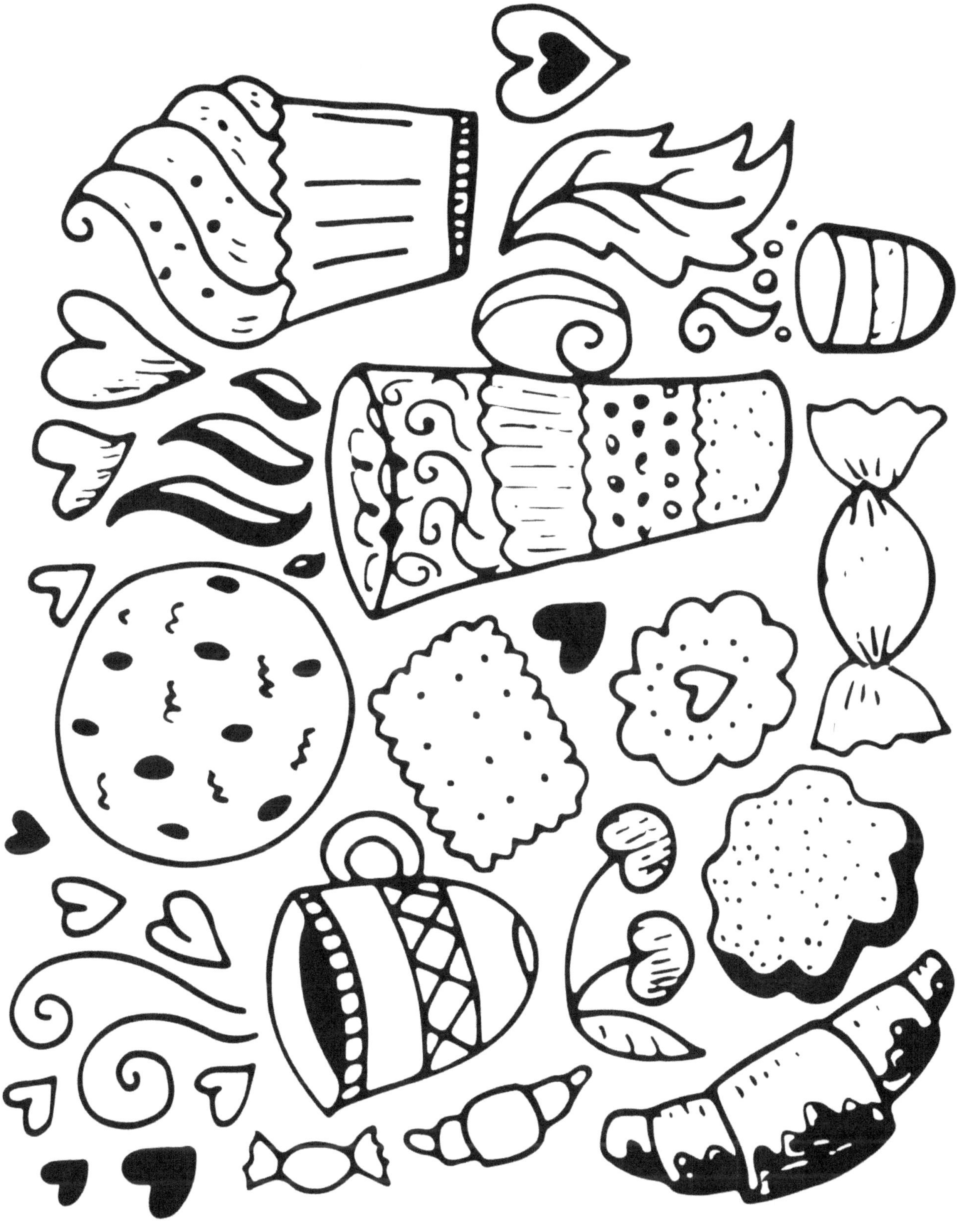

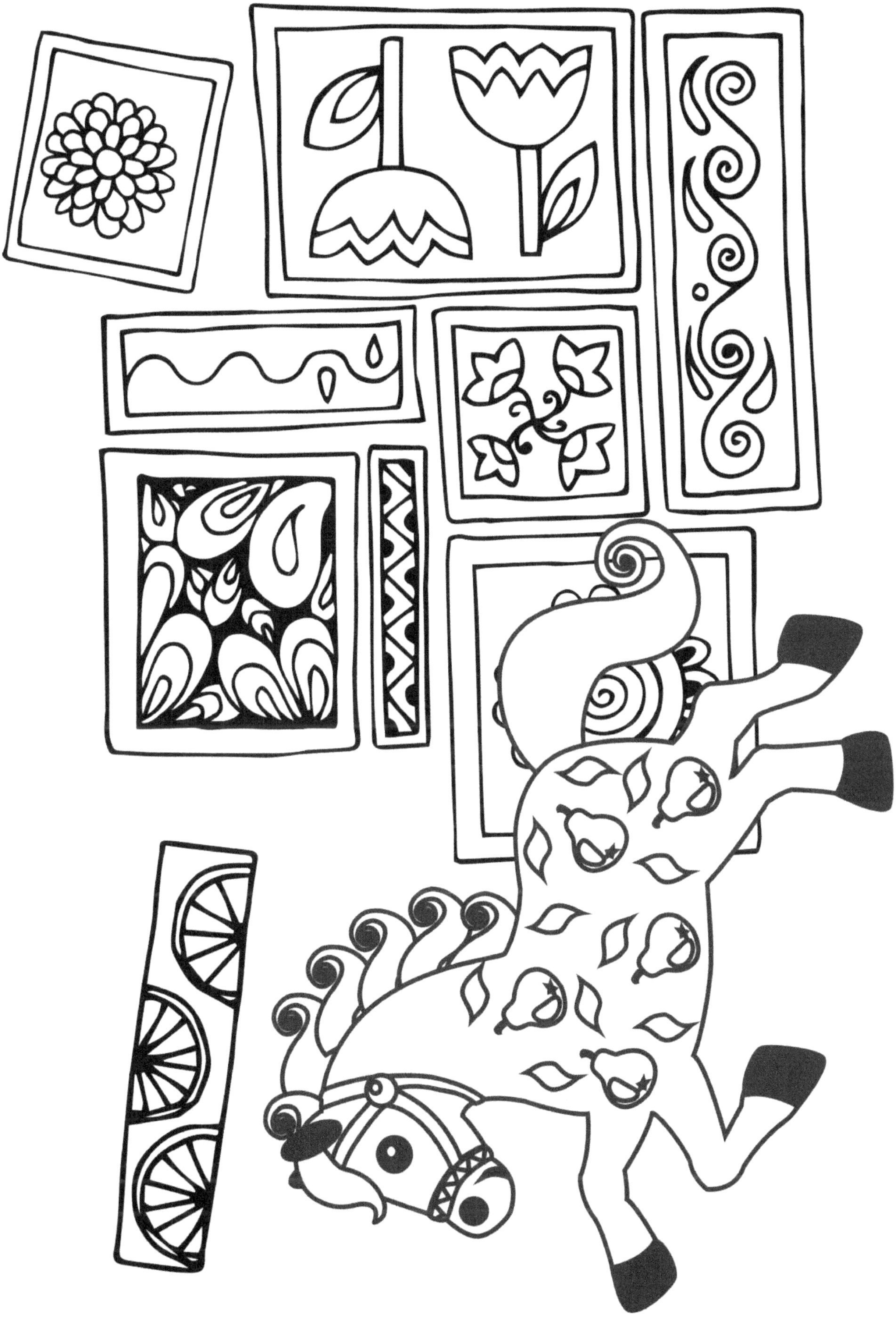

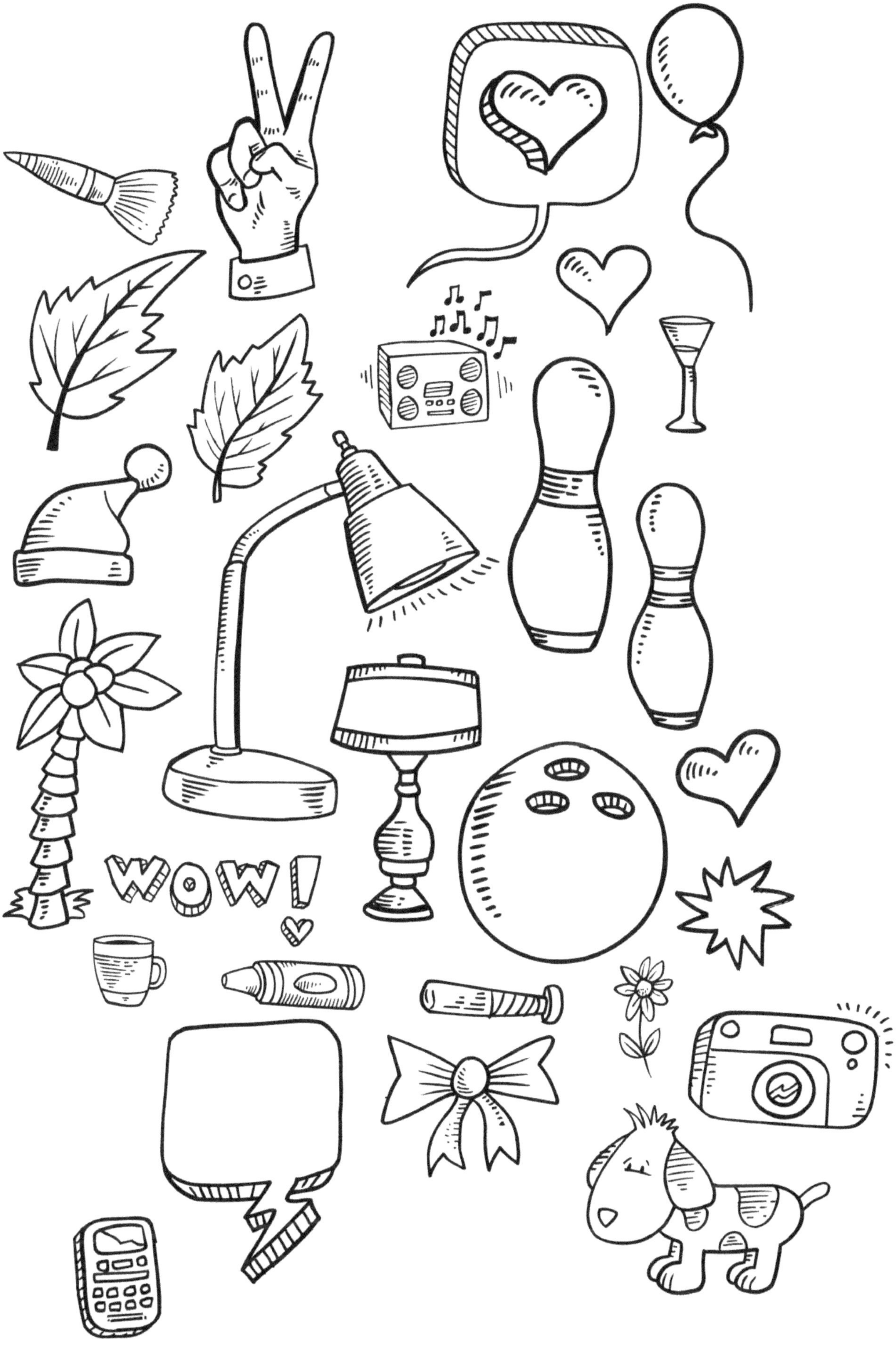
WOW!

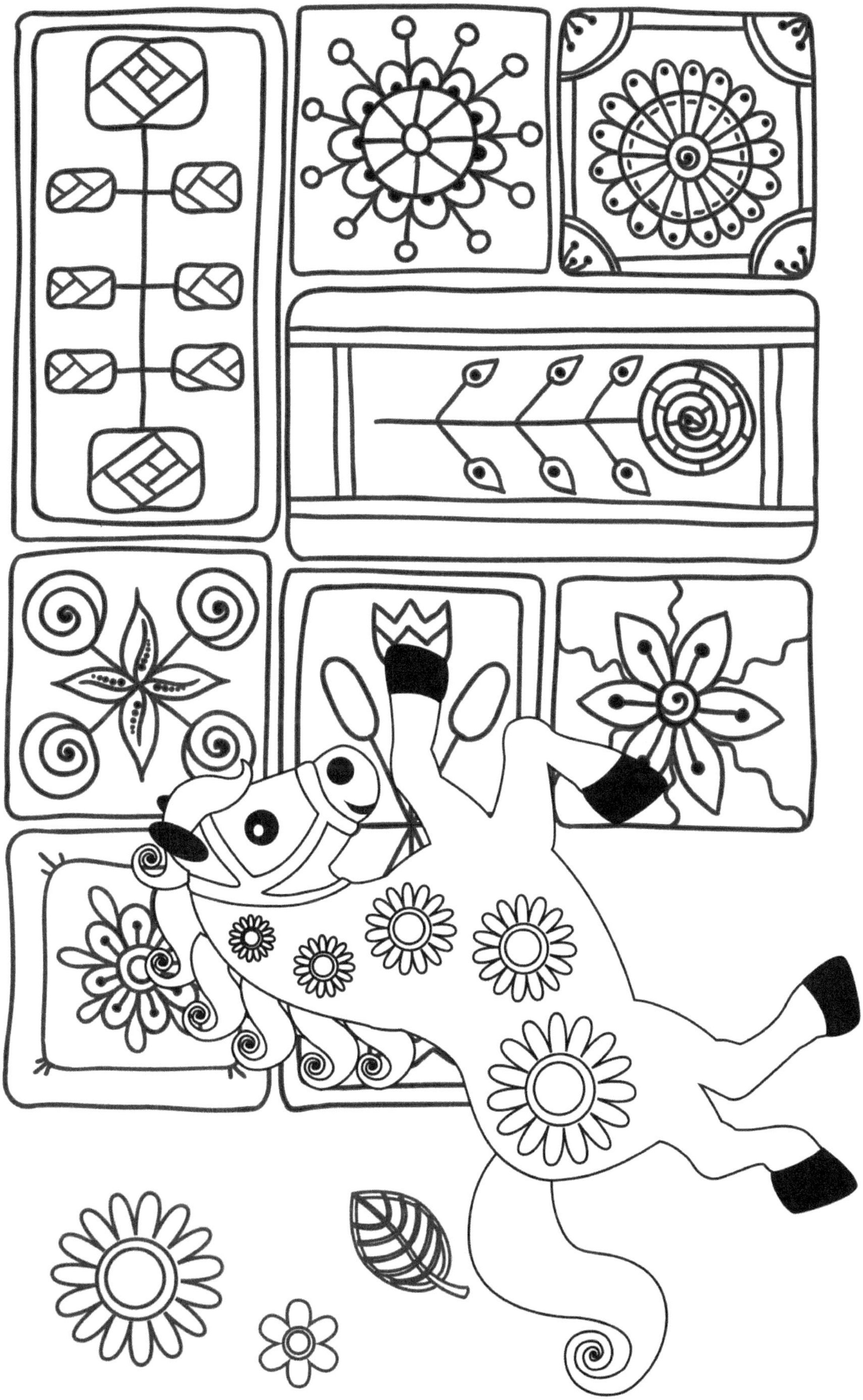

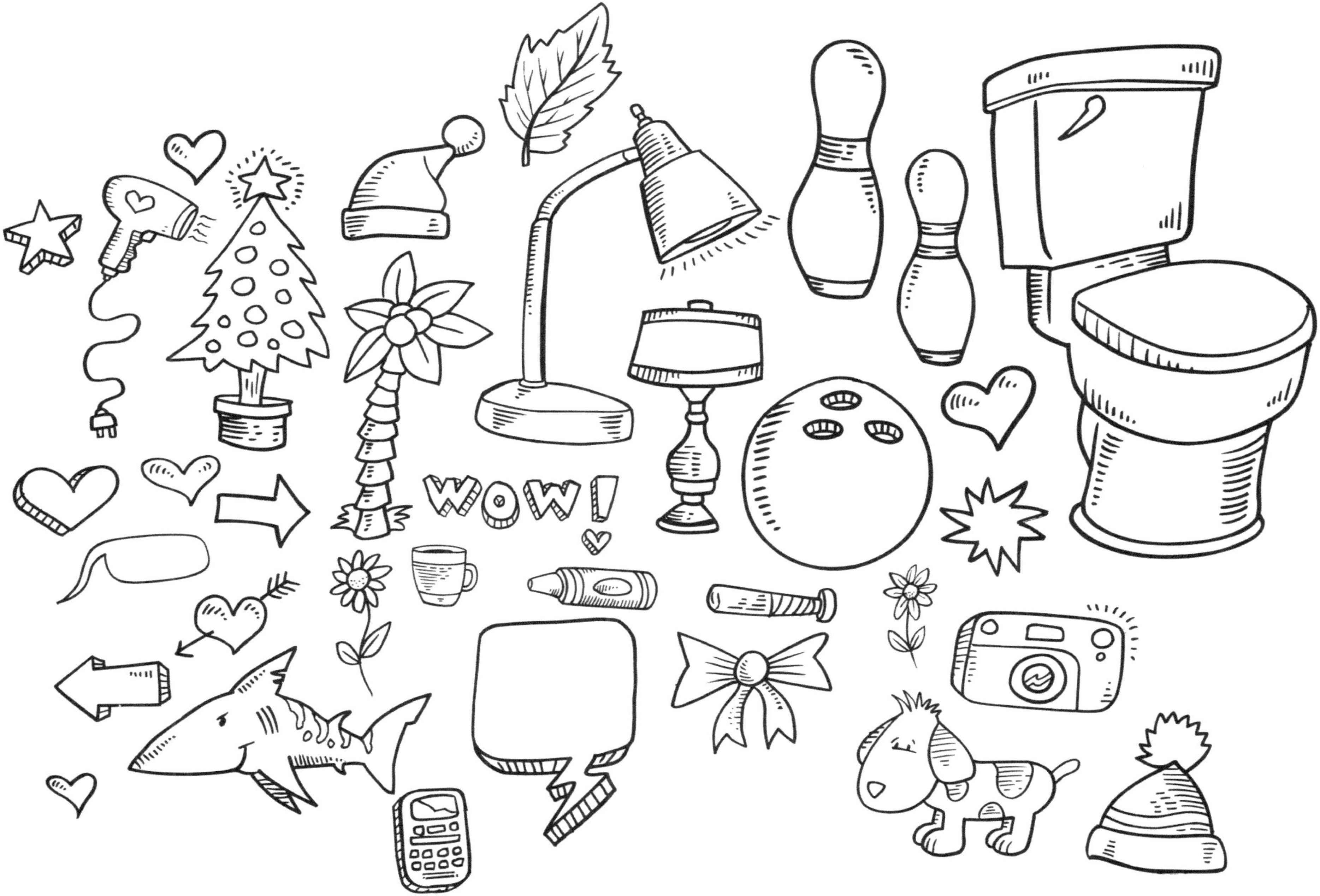
WOW!

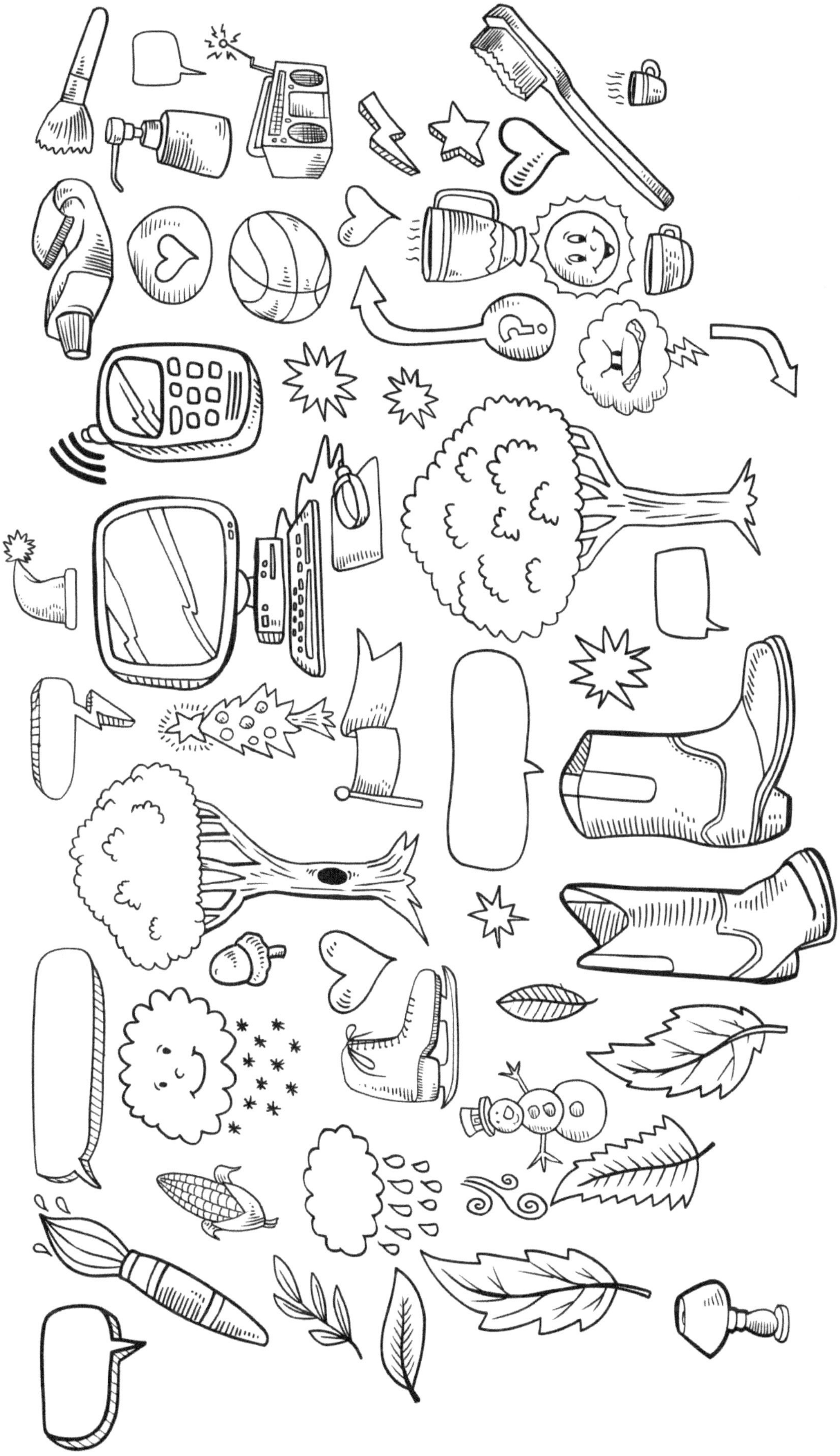

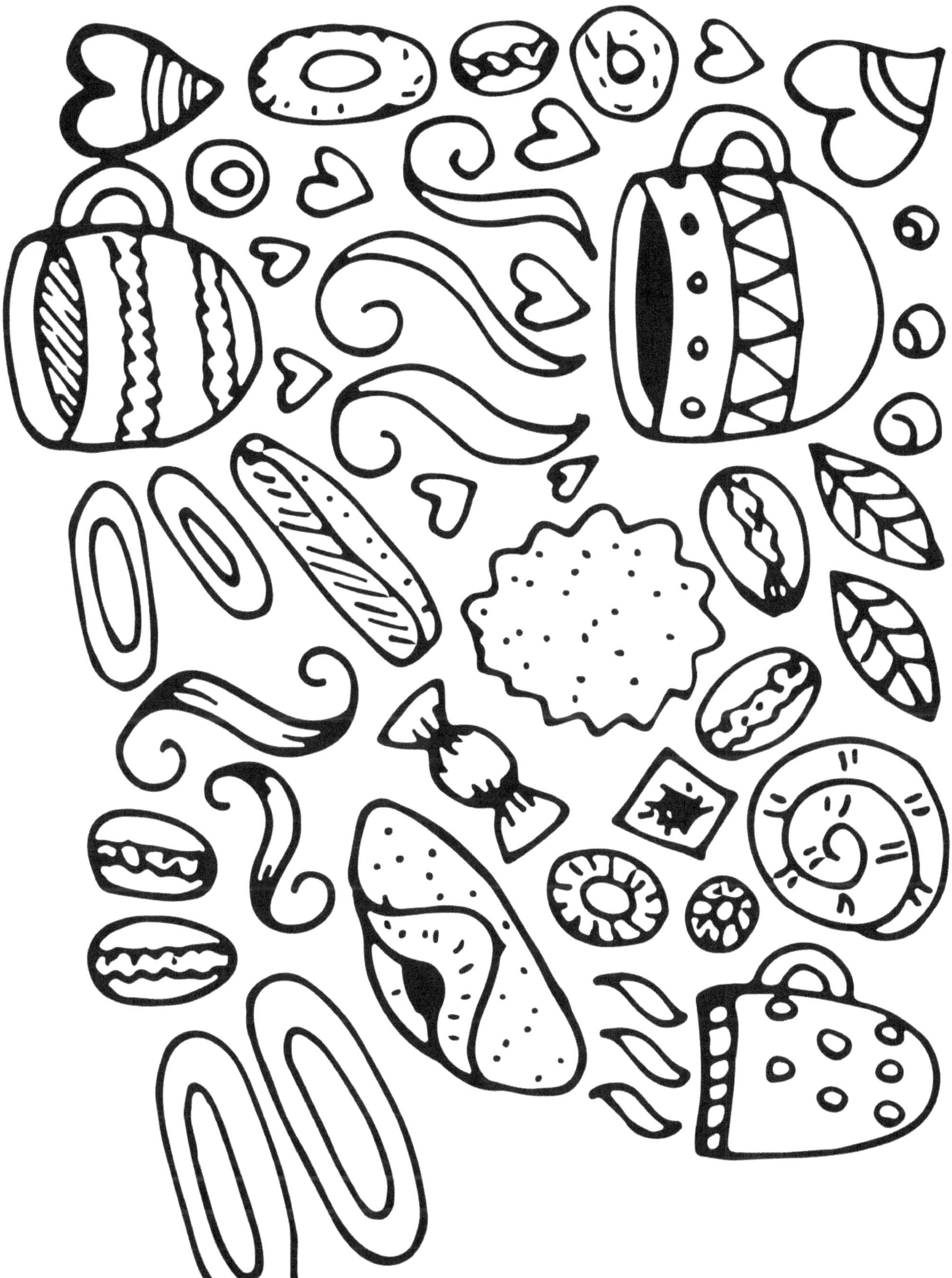

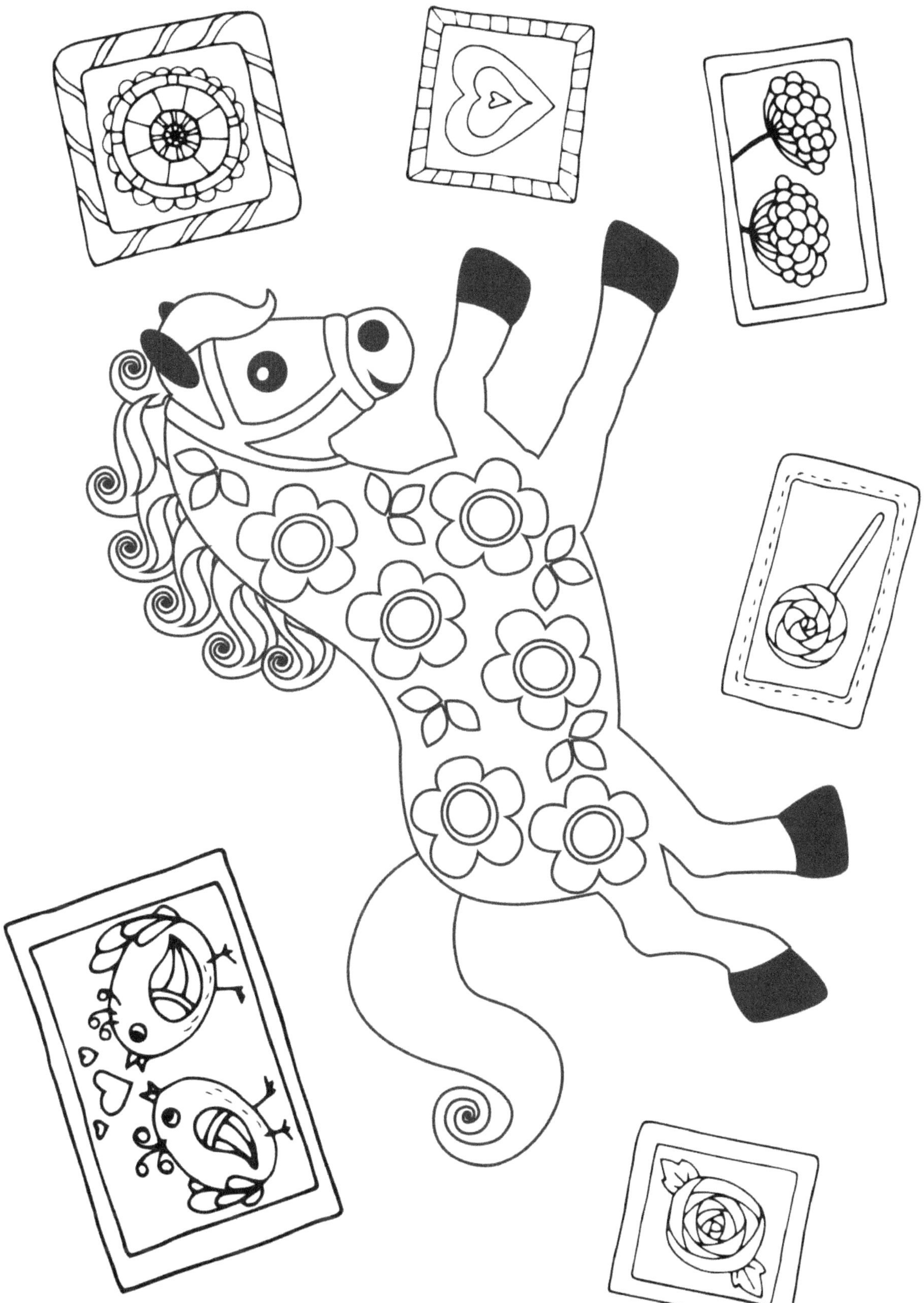

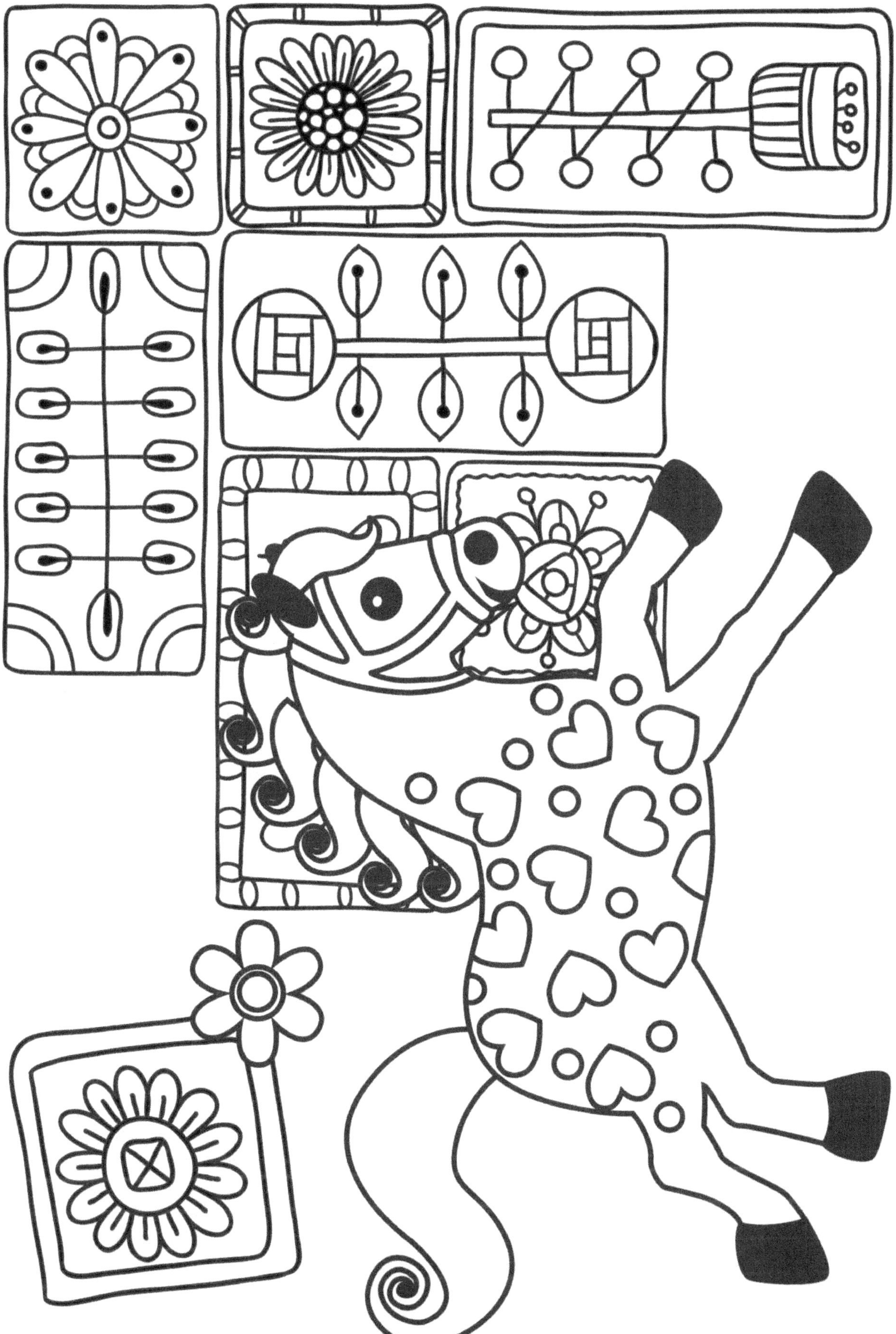

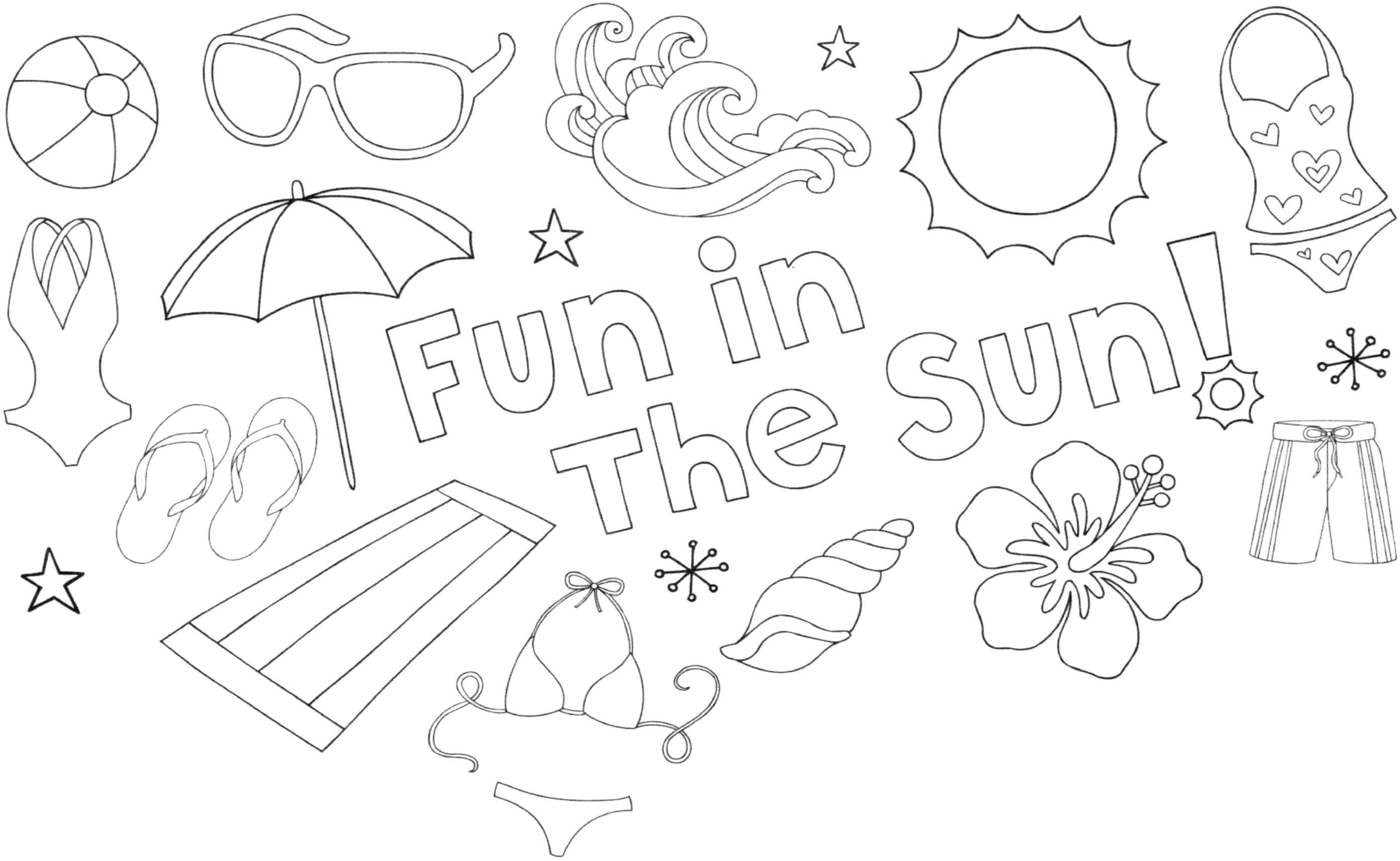
Fun in
The Sun!